D0765407

Winning Tactics for Weekend Singles

OTHER JOE HYAMS TENNIS BOOKS

Winning Tactics for Weekend Tennis,
with Tony Trabert
Billie Jean King's Secrets of Winning Tennis,
with Billie Jean King

Winning Tactics for Weekend Singles

Pancho Gonzales and Joe Hyams

Holt, Rinehart and Winston

New York   Chicago   San Francisco

Published simultaneously in Canada by Holt, Rinehart
and Winston of Canada, Limited.

Library of Congress Cataloging in Publication Data
Gonzales, Pancho, date.
Winning tactics for weekend singles.
1. Tennis – Miscellanea.   I. Hyams, Joseph, joint
author.   II. Title.
GV995.G65   796.34'22   74-4808
ISBN 0-03-013136-7

Photographs by John Hamilton, Globe Photos, Inc.

First Edition

Printed in the United States of America

CONTENTS

Winning Tactics for Weekend Singles

1.
PRELIMINARIES | *Lessons*

What is the best age to start learning how to play tennis?

I feel that children under the age of twelve are too young to start with athletics because they don't have the necessary stamina. Also, a child under the age of twelve usually doesn't have the mental capability of handling and retaining the details of shots, tactics, and psychology of tennis. Some parents start their children off at the age of eight, but the game is often too much for them and they tend to get bored with it quickly. I'd rather see an eight-year-old play on a miniature tennis court with a paddle or start as I did with handball and learn hand and eye coordination first.

However, a lot depends on the youngster's physical capability and interest in the game. I started my son Richard, Jr., at ten, but he showed a natural ability from the start and had grown up in a tennis-oriented environment.

I was twelve and a half when I started playing tennis, and within six months I had won some tournaments. By the time I was fourteen I was the fifteen-and-under champion for Southern California. But I was already a qualified handball player, using both hands, and I had played a lot of paddleball. My eye was trained and I had a knowledge of ball bounce.

1

At what age is someone too old to start playing tennis?

That depends on the individual. If someone has led a sedentary life and starts playing tennis at fifty, there's no reason why he can't take some lessons and go out and hit on an instructional basis. He should also play some doubles with a partner who can run a bit so when he is up at the net he doesn't have to be concerned about moving back.

On the other hand there are exceptions. I have a friend who recently started playing at a late age. He did the whole bit: he bought movies and books and had me give him personal instruction. Although I didn't believe he would learn much, I never saw anyone of his age so enthusiastic about the game. Now, he hits the ball very well but has no idea of how to win points.

Of course, he is in fine physical condition, but before he started the game I had him visit his doctor and continue getting occasional checkups to be certain the game was not too hard on him.

A man with an athletic background stays in shape one way or another and there's no reason why such a man, whether he is in his fifties or sixties, can't enjoy weekend doubles and occasional singles with someone who plays his caliber game.

Do you have any special advice for the older person?

Before starting tennis see a doctor for a complete checkup. Then take lessons and start off reasonably slowly, giving the body time to adjust to the exercise. Most important, never get into a fiercely competitive situation, especially when you are playing against someone younger. Your mind may not have slowed down but your body does, and an older person must realize and accept the fact that he is not a kid anymore.

How do you suggest a beginner learn how to play tennis?

Most areas of the country have public school tennis clinics for adults as well as children during the summer months. The clinics are a good way to start because they bring a group of beginners together at one place and everyone is more or less at the same level of play. A lot of beginners are shy and timid about going on the court with better players, but in a clinic setting they can find a number of willing partners. This is important because the students can develop confidence and as they improve they can then try to get into games at a slightly higher level of play.

I especially like the clinics for youngsters because they move the learner at a slower pace than does a private instructor, and a student's mind will retain more of what is being talked about. The student also develops a mental picture as the instructor demonstrates, and he has a lot of other youngsters his age to talk to and play with. It's more like a fun event than a lesson, which can sometimes be dull.

When I was teaching youngsters I usually gave lessons to four of them at once, over a period of an hour. While I instructed one pair, the other pair practiced what they had learned on another court. I always asked the entire group to practice together at least once a week so they could refresh their memories and strokes.

A similar system would probably work well for a group of four adults, who could share the cost of a one-hour lesson. Most adults will find that by listening and by watching the mistakes of other learners, they can gain almost as much knowledge as in a private lesson.

Another good way to learn is to go to public tennis courts and watch people play. About twelve or thirteen years ago, at Exposition Park in Los Angeles, a group of men in their late fifties and sixties used to sit around and watch us practice. They knew all the players and we knew them, but I never saw any of them play tennis during the ten or fifteen years we practiced there.

One year I went away on tour and when I got back to the courts I saw four or five of those same men playing. They had simply decided to play, and I was amazed at how well they hit the ball. Obviously, all the observing they had done had developed in their minds an idea of what they wanted to do and how to do it. They laid the racket back properly and hit the ball over the net.

They weren't taking lessons — they didn't have to. Their success proved to me that one of the best ways to learn is to watch and then imitate. Within a year they were playing pretty good tennis.

When I was learning how to play, I used to watch a fellow named Willis Anderson who was very fast on the court. He had a long pointy nose, and whenever he ran for a ball his nose was right down on the ground and he hit every ball from an extreme

4

crouch. I watched him for months and even walked around in a crouch and started to exaggerate my movements on the court. I believe that the first preparation for movement is the crouch position and by copying Anderson I became much quicker off the mark.

What do you think of tennis camps for young-sters?

My feeling is that parents who want their young-ster to play tennis should consider sending the child to a tennis camp at least once a year. The average fee for three weeks is about $500, which may seem expensive, but if a youngster goes to a tennis camp once a year from the time he's twelve years old until he's seventeen, he will know the game well enough to be able to enjoy it tremen-dously for the rest of his life. And, if he cares to, he can take his tennis to the highest level he is capa-ble of reaching.

I feel the money spent is a good investment for a youngster. He may not realize the pleasure of ten-nis at the time, but when he gets a bit older he will have the basics of a sport that will provide him with pleasure for a lifetime.

There's another factor. People have often told me they wished they had started playing tennis earlier because later in life their muscles took on certain tendencies and they no longer had the flexibility to learn the basic strokes. I feel it is better to develop the capability early, even if it is not followed up, rather than wait until you are unable to train the muscles properly.

What about television as a learning aid?

Television can be a first-rate instructional guide if the viewer studies the game and the players rather than sitting glued to the set interested only in the outcome.

Too often spectators watch the flight of the ball and never actually study the player's stroke and footwork and how quickly he recovers his position.

You can always learn from better players by watching them and trying to imitate their ways of stroking the ball. You will always fall into your own natural stance because you are probably built differently from the person you are imitating, but at least you will have a concept of how the shot or stroke should be made.

How do you suggest choosing an instructor?

Instructors like myself, Alex Olmedo, Pancho Segura, and other professionals are not so different from average players such as my assistant at Caesar's Palace, Chuck Pate. Chuck taught me how to play tennis. He was never a champion but in 1942 he was able to teach me certain ideas of the game I still use today. Most instructors are good for anyone but tournament players, who require very special assistance.

As a rule I have found that good young players don't have the patience or the desire to be good teachers. They would rather play and they often hit too hard to be working with beginners. Generally speaking, the older teachers will give you more for your money.

Preliminaries

Should I change instructors?

It may be time to change when your instructor is merely hitting the ball with you or you feel you aren't getting enough out of your lessons. But you should be honest with yourself. Do you really want more instruction or are you satisfied with having someone hit with you and give you exercise and occasional pointers?

It's possible, however, that you have learned as much as your instructor can offer. Many teachers are not capable of handling more advanced players and there's no reason for you not to seek out one of the top professionals in your area and ask him if he thinks you can learn from him. You'll usually get an honest answer.

A good instructor will advance you as time passes. He will make you run harder and faster and get you to hit more balls. And he will probably intimidate you a little because in order to benefit from instruction you have to work harder. If you feel yourself improving, you probably have a good teacher and there's no reason to change.

In any event, I think it's a good idea occasionally to receive instruction from other teachers: if they're good you'll learn from them, and if they're bad you'll also learn.

But before you seek out other teachers be aware of your capabilities and style of play and don't allow anyone to change your style radically. Too many teachers want the student to play as they do, and since we all are built differently, we all have to play differently.

*Do you recommend half-hour or one-hour les-
sons?*

I don't think that a one-hour lesson is of much
value to a beginner because he won't be able to retain everything that is told or shown to him.

I believe most people would be wiser taking two
half-hour lessons a week rather than one hour-long
lesson. During each half-hour you should concentrate on just one thing — otherwise it's too confus-
ing. The spaced exercise of the half-hour sessions
will be a benefit and you will have time between
lessons to practice what you have learned.

There are so many shots and so many stances in
tennis that if a learner is given too much in one
lesson he will become confused. It's far wiser to let
each stroke flow gradually into the next.

*What about lessons that change or improve a
stroke?*

My approach as a teacher is not to change a
stroke but to add a stroke. For example, if a person
has an underslice backhand, I will usually say to
him, "You already know how to hit an underslice
backhand, so we are not going to work on that at
all. What we're going to do is give you a flat backhand so you will have two different types of backhand."

Too often an instructor will say, "That's a lousy
backhand you have. You should hit it flat." The instructor takes away the student's confidence in one
stroke, which may be ingrained and occasionally

successful, and tries to give him something new which may not work, thus destroying his confidence in his backhand. I believe it's much wiser to teach him to hit a second shot instead of taking away the first.

Sometimes it's better to help a person develop his unorthodox shot into something better. For example, Carl Earn, a top-ranking player of the forties, had a left-handed forehand which was one of the best shots I've ever seen. He laid the racket far back and as he hit the ball, he shot the racket straight up for the moon. That stroke went against all the basic rules of the game, but had somebody tried to change it, they would have ruined it. Earn worked with what he had and perfected it, and the stroke became one of the best forehand shots in the game even though it was slightly unorthodox.

I wouldn't take a thirty-year-old student, who has been playing for two or three years, and try to fool him by saying I am going to make a champion out of him. All I can do is work with and improve what he already has so he will get more satisfaction out of the game. If I tried to change him, I would only mix him up and take away his confidence.

On some occasions as a teacher, I find it useful to move the student around the court more in order to make him do a little more than he thinks he can. At the same time I study him to be certain he's not getting too tired. I have often found, however, that when a student thinks he is tired he simply must grit his teeth, bear down, and perhaps get a little angry for five or ten minutes. By pushing himself harder he will discover he can really do more than he thought was possible. This is the major difference between a champion and a runner-up.

Is there a standard way of playing tennis?

There's no standard way of playing, particularly for the social player. You end up at whatever level your skill and physical capability permit. If you have a good start with the proper fundamentals you have a better chance of going farther than if you start late and your game develops some bad habits.

There's no basic way of playing because everyone is built differently, so you should try to develop your own abilities. A person who can run the 100-yard dash in 9.8 seconds is going to be a far different tennis player than one who runs the dash in 11 seconds. One man gets to the ball sooner and the other man a little later. Each man therefore must have a different position on the court depending on his speed of foot. This is where the age factor comes in. It explains why an older person can't play as well as someone younger.

Do you believe there are any advantages to learning a two-handed stroke?

No, and especially not for anyone who ultimately wants to play competitive tennis. Even with the recent victories of Chris Evert and Jimmy Connors at Wimbledon, it has still to be proved that a two-handed stroke has any special advantages.

Today's youngsters can learn how to play tennis with a shorter racket, so there's no need for them to start off with a heavy racket as did most two-handed players, including Pancho Segura, who was the best of the lot. When Segura was a little boy he used his father's heavy racket and the only way he could manage it was with both hands. But, he was very quick getting to his ground strokes, and when he got to the net he volleyed with one hand. Most two-handed players are not as good as he was at net.

I don't recommend that an older player learn a two-handed stroke because he would have to be exceptionally fast on his feet in order to get into position for many shots. Of course, there are people who must use two hands on the racket because of a physical defect or lack of strength.

Will playing tennis affect my golf game?

I've played golf for years whenever I had spare time and I consistently shoot in the low eighties. For the most part I think the exercise a golfer gets from tennis benefits his overall game by keeping him more physically fit.

More and more professionals from other sports are now taking up tennis, including football players such as Deacon Jones, Jim Brown, Mike Garrett, and O. J. Simpson, basketballer Gail Goodrich, miler Jim Ryun, pole-vaulter Bob Seagren, hockey player Rod Gilbert of the New York Rangers, light-heavyweight boxing champion Bob Foster, and even the legendary pitcher Satchel Paige. The list is endless and I hope they all truly enjoy the game.

The Racket

What weight do you suggest for the racket?

Obviously that depends on the individual. A person with a long arm will probably find he is more comfortable with a lighter racket because the arc of his swing is long enough to give him the necessary power and leverage. Someone who is shorter or stubbier can use a heavier racket because he usually has a stronger arm and doesn't have to swing it as far — he may want the racket to do a little more of the work.

I do feel that most average and beginning players are using rackets that are too heavy. Although I play tennis almost every day, I find that a 13¼-ounce racket (strung) is a little too heavy for me, so you can imagine how heavy a 14- or 15-ounce racket must feel in the average player's hand.

I weigh my rackets right down to the gram, which is an extreme, but since my hobby is automobile racing, in which we balance everything, I have the proper weighing equipment. I normally use a racket that weighs about 13 ounces strung, maximum 13½ ounces, and after about three sets I can handle only a 12¾-ounce racket. The reason I prefer such a light racket is that my arm is not as strong as it used to be and I like to delay the action of my shot, to disguise it as long as possible and still be able to get the racket around in time. I try to make up for the lack of weight in the racket by using a thinner-gauge gut.

12

RULE OF THUMB: Any racket under 12½ or 13 ounces is probably too light for the average man, but anything over 13½ or 14 ounces is probably too heavy. A woman should also use a lighter racket. Billie Jean King, for example, uses a 13¼ ounce racket—the same weight as mine.

There is, however, a use for a slightly heavier racket. Sometimes I train for a match with a heavier racket than the one I am planning to use. Then two or three days before the tournament I go back to my lighter racket in order to get the feel of the balance and weight, and my hand always feels stronger. I don't actually play with the heavier racket. In effect, I use it to build up strength in my arm.

Which is better: wood or metal?

The difference between wood and metal rackets is that the ball will leave the metal racket earlier, so you don't have as much time to control the ball as you do with wood. Therefore, the older player who needs to have a little more zip in his shots might benefit from metal.

Many of today's top players have gone back to wood because they like to see the ball go where they aim it. Also, they prefer to swing harder because that gives them a better rhythm.

I suggest that a young player start with wood because it will give him the strength in his arm that he needs to become a good player.

I must say, however, that the difference between wood and metal is really academic for the most part. I've always maintained that if I were to blindfold a player he wouldn't know whether he was playing with wood or metal.

Do you recommend an evenly balanced racket or one that is heavier in the head?

I've always felt that the weight of the racket should be where it makes contact — in the head. For example, if a racket weighs 13 ounces, I prefer it to weigh 7 ounces from the center point to the tip of the head and 6 ounces from the center point to the handle. Most metal rackets are evenly weighted, and to make the head a trifle heavier, I used $1/8$-ounce adhesive lead weights, which can be bought at any golf store. Four or five of these weights taped on the head of the racket will usually run the weight up enough to make the difference.

Will I have problems changing from a heavier racket to a lighter one?

When people change from a heavy racket to one that is lighter they find they can whip the light racket through the ball a little quicker, so obviously they lose some control. What you have to do is carry the lighter racket through a little farther and give yourself a week or two of practice with it. Chances are you will find that you swing better and get more power with the lighter racket and, eventually, get more deception.

What size handle do you recommend?

I feel that the maximum size anyone should use is a handle that is 4¾ inches in circumference. Personally I use a grip that is between 4½ and 4⅝ inches. Racket manufacturers are now coming out with a grip 4⅜ inches in circumference, which will probably feel more comfortable in a lady's or youngster's hand.

How can I determine the proper-size handle?

A good way of choosing the proper size is to find a racket that doesn't slip in your hand. If it's too large the racket will twist in your hand because you can't grip it firmly. If you get a racket with a grip that is too small, the skin will wrinkle on your hand and that will create a blister. It's important to get the right grip and stay with it because your hand becomes grooved to it.

What shape do you suggest for the grip?

I prefer a rectangular shape because the flatter part lies more in the palm of the hand than on the side. And I think the rectangular shape gives the beginner a better idea of where his hand should be and where the racket is.

Do you suggest nylon or gut for the average weekend player?

There's no reason in the world why anyone should want to use gut rather than nylon, unless they have been playing for many years. Nylon is not affected by the weather; it's less expensive; it will play just as well as gut and for the most part it wears longer.

The beginning player who wants to save money will get just as much out of his game from nylon as he will from gut, but he should have his racket strung just a little tighter initially because nylon tends to lose some of its tension over a period of time.

Gut is more sensitive than nylon, and if you break one string the whole string job loses its tension. Even after repair it isn't the same. All things considered, I don't see much benefit in using gut for the weekend player. Pros use it because they get a 2 or 3 percent advantage on the speed of the ball, but that percentage is so low that only a pro can tell the difference.

What gauge of gut do you recommend for the player who is determined to use gut?

Gauges of gut come in different thicknesses: 15, 15 light, 16, 16 light, 17, and 17 light. The higher the number, the thinner the gut and the quicker it wears out. I recommend 16½ light for tournament play because most players will get more speed from it than the more frequently used 15 gauge. I use 17 gauge light when I play in competition, but I usually wear out an entire string job each time I play a match. A player who decides to switch to a thinner gut should give himself time to get used to it because suddenly a ball that has been just reaching the baseline will be going past it.

How tight should a racket be strung?

It's very rare that anyone uses a board-tight racket because the strings then lose their sling-shot effect and therefore their power.

I think that a tightly strung racket (about 65 pounds) is probably a little too tight for the weekend player. I suggest a medium-tight racket, which ranges from 55 to 60 pounds. Then the ball will stay on the racket a little longer.

Professionally speaking, my views on string jobs are also based on other factors: the weight of the ball, the condition of the court, the moisture in the air, and the altitude. If the ball is extremely soft, I would use less tension in my racket so that when the ball hits the strings it doesn't flatten out so much. It will retain a relatively round form. But if the ball is soft or you are playing at a high altitude, the ball will come into a tightly strung racket, flatten out like an egg, and then porpoise through the air.

Practice

How much practice or playing time can the average weekend player handle comfortably?

More than you realize if you want to organize your time schedule. If your interest in the game is strong and keeping yourself in condition is important, you can find the time for tennis. As a weekend player you should try to play once in the middle of the week for at least an hour, if you want to improve your game, because the five-day lag between the weekends will slow your progress. If you are able to go out twice during the week for a half-hour tune-up each time, that's even better. Some people claim they can't take the time, but I believe they could if they wanted to and the result would be beneficial for both health and business. Running in the evening will also help your conditioning.

Over the years, in knowing a lot of businessmen who play tennis, I have found that those who play religiously stay in the best physical condition. A friend of mine who is in business used to lunch at a tennis club and made it a point to conduct some of his business meetings there. He would play tennis for an hour before lunch, have a light lunch at the club with business associates, and then go back to his office. He took a two-hour lunch break but when he returned to the office his mind and body were refreshed and he told me he was able to do more work than he could have done without the exercise.

In the sixties while I was in Washington conducting instructional clinics, I was invited to Robert Kennedy's home for social doubles at 7:00 in the morning. On the morning of the game I thought to myself, "This is crazy. I've never been up at 7 A.M. to play with anybody."

But when I arrived at his house I was directed right to the tennis court and found him and some of his staff sweeping the court and wiping up the dew. We started playing and I thoroughly enjoyed the game because I thought it was great that anyone got up so early just to get in a little tennis.

After the game, at about 9:30, we were invited in to breakfast, and while we were sitting at the table Mr. Kennedy rushed upstairs and returned in a few minutes, having showered and dressed for the office, where he was due at 10:00.

I found out later that the early-morning tennis was part of his daily routine. He enjoyed playing, liked the exercise, and managed to squeeze it in by getting up a little earlier in the morning.

What if you don't have a partner for practice?

A ball machine can be great for practice. I've used one and so have many other pros and top players.

When I was a youngster, I would hit a ball against a garage door and I found it very good practice. If you do that I suggest that rather than mix the shots up, from backhand to forehand, you concentrate on the forehand for a while, trying to hit the ball with a perfect stroke. That type of training also helps strengthen the arm a bit, and it should help you get into the habit of focusing on the ball as it makes contact with the racket. Then later concentrate on your backhand. You might also buy an inexpensive rebound net or backboard that would allow you to get a fine workout in the driveway of your home.

Do you recommend any kind of practice routine?

If most people reversed their normal practice routine they would probably improve some of their deficient strokes and have a more balanced game.

For instance, the hardest shot for the average player to hit is the overhead, which is also the least practiced. The second hardest shot is the serve, because it's rarely practiced enough, and the third hardest shot is the volley for the same reason — not enough practice. The easiest shots for most people are the backhand and forehand, because they are used the most frequently.

That's why I recommend a reversal of the normal routine. Usually players who are on the court for practice start hitting forehands and backhands. They hit perhaps a hundred of each before moving up to the net and hitting perhaps twenty-five or thirty volleys on both sides, and then two or three overheads and a half-dozen serves.

People just don't equalize their practice time, which is one of the reasons most of them have difficulty with the least-practiced shots.

Should I practice a stroke I am learning during a game?

No. In competition you are trying to make the best possible use of those strokes you have mastered and that is not the time to work on undeveloped ones. You will only get discouraged and uptight and probably get into bad habits if you try strokes that you cannot handle. In competition, I suggest you always emphasize your strength and build your game around it. All of the great players have done just that!

How much practice does a serious player require?

A minimum of five hours a day of good hard practice. The best program is to divide the practice into two sessions: morning and afternoon. The morning session should be used for loosening up, leaving the heavy practice and serious playing until the afternoon.

Even when I don't feel like playing tennis I force myself to go out and take the time to play because I know when I am finished with the session I'll feel better. And the more balls I hit, the better I will play.

Is it all right to practice with old balls?

Whenever possible I feel the learner should use good balls for practicing. I know that many teachers use old balls for instruction sessions, but then the student must realize that the flight of an old ball may not be consistent. The stroke is the critical measure. A student may make a good stroke but the ball may go astray simply because it is too light. So you should not be overly critical of yourself when you are hitting old balls. Just concentrate on making the proper stroke.

Is it advisable to hit the ball on the second bounce during practice sessions?

While you're warming up it is all right to hit on the second bounce, but as soon as the blood starts flowing and the body loosens up you should attempt to hit the ball on the first bounce. During a practice session you want to react as you would during a game, and that means hitting the ball on the first bounce.

If you have only an hour or two to play each week, do you think it is wiser to play a game or to practice?

I think a little of both is good for everyone, even beginners, because in competitive play you always extend yourself more. But the beginner should devote more time to practice than to playing, to give himself a chance to groove his strokes so he won't falter under tension.

As a golfing enthusiast I have a problem common to most weekend tennis players. I'd rather be out playing eighteen holes but, knowing the value of practice, I make it a point to occasionally hit two or three buckets of golf balls. This gives me a chance to focus my eyes on the ball and feel the head of the club meeting the ball.

How about playing in tournaments?

Parents frequently ask me what they can do for a youngster who wants to improve his game. If he already has good strokes I suggest he enter all of the tournaments at his level of play.

I feel that tournaments are good for everyone because you learn to play under tension against different people. It's fun, win or lose, and in many cases a player will learn as much from losing as he will from winning.

Pregame

How can someone get back to playing tennis after a long absence from the game?

Let's say that someone who played tennis when he was a kid and who is now a forty-year-old businessman decides he wants to pick up the game again. He's not going to be able to go out on the first day and play as he did twenty-five years earlier, and he had better be aware of it. On that first day he should do some limbering up exercises and, if possible, take a half-hour lesson to regroove his strokes. The next time he goes out he should play for half an hour and gradually build up his playing time over a period of weeks.

The first few days are the disaster days—the period when he will be stiff and tired and will have to force himself to play. By the end of the first week he will find he has started to build up stamina again. Within a month he ought to be able to play a full hour without any strain.

Unless he is in good physical condition, however, I don't advise him to play competitive singles, particularly if he is the type of person who feels he has to win. Too many men who think nothing of losing thousands of dollars on a business transaction will put tremendous strain on their nerves and their heart in order to win a point in a friendly game.

The person who wants to get back into shape for serious playing should follow a slightly different regimen. I recommend that he play half an hour each day for the first week and gradually increase his time over a period of a month until he is playing an hour or more daily. It's always a good idea to stop playing while you still feel like continuing rather than to wait until you are dog-tired.

Do you suggest that a player get into shape for tennis by working out with weights or exercising at a gymnasium?

I don't believe in weight lifting for tennis, which is a game of endurance, speed, and timing more than one of pure strength. I don't have an especially strong hand and my wrists are probably not as strong as a weight lifter's. But I have learned the secret of timing and weight transfer to give me power. If weights were important, how could a player like Ken Rosewall, who has never lifted a weight in his life, hit the ball as hard as he does?

Also I feel that weight lifting can restrict your ease of movement, reflexes, and speed, and can make you tense instead of loose.

Visits to a gym can be useful, however, if you do overall calisthenics and some rope jumping. You can also practice the Australian jump in which your knees come up to your chest.

Running sprints is an excellent conditioner, as is a proper diet, low in carbohydrates.

But the best exercise and conditioning for tennis are what you get on the court, if you force yourself to run and move around and improve your footwork.

Is it all right to eat before playing?

Speaking for myself, I never eat anything for at least three hours before a game because I like to give my nervous system a chance to relax. I feel most players would be well advised not to eat or to eat very lightly before an important game.

What about taking a nap before playing?

I sometimes nap for one or two hours before a big match. I may not sleep for the entire time but at some point I will get about three-quarters of an hour of sleep and when I awaken my eyes are rested and I feel I can lift a house.

I consider a nap after a game important as a refresher if you feel you have extended yourself.

Is sex before playing harmful?

There has been a lot written pro and con about this subject, with most of the emphasis on the negative side. If a player has sex every night for a week prior to a Davis Cup match he's going to be in trouble on that intense afternoon of the game. I would even say that having sex on the day before a match is a mistake. This is one of the areas of sacrifice and discipline that go with being a champion. However, I believe that having sex two or three days prior to a match can help relax your nervous system.

What kind of weather do you think is best for the older player?

At the age of forty-five I consider myself an older player and I like hot weather. About two or three years ago, when I was coaching the Mexican Davis Cup team in Mexico City, I got a stiffness in my neck and was unable to turn my head around for several days. Luckily I work at Caesar's Palace, and when I returned to Las Vegas the temperature was around 110 degrees. After eight hours of just walking around in the sunlight I lost my stiffness.

Is there any way to prevent blisters?

Blisters on the hand are often caused by using the wrong-size racket handle. If the handle is too small the skin on your hand will wrinkle up and create a blister. So be certain that the racket handle is large enough to allow a firm and proper grip.

If you have not played tennis for several months, it is to be expected that you will get some small blisters on the palm of your hand, near the thumb and on the balls of your fingers, because of the friction in these areas and the fact that your skin has not been toughened yet.

You can help prevent these blisters either by resuming play slowly and carefully, or by wearing a chamois tennis or golf glove every other day to give your hand a chance to rest. There are even some players who wear a chamois glove all the time because they say it helps them get a firmer grip on the racket.

There's another reason for blisters on the hand. You may be holding onto the racket throughout a game as if it meant life or death to you. Dennis Ralston, former Davis Cup champion, always had blisters, and I used to tell him not to take his tension out on the racket, and to relax.

You should hold the racket just firmly enough so that no one can pull it out of your hand, and only as you make contact with the ball should you put a life or death grip on the racket. Since my hands don't perspire quite as much as they used to, and perspiration is a sort of lubricant, whenever I see the skin on my hand getting a little dry I tape up those spots as a precautionary measure.

Painful blisters on the feet can be caused by wearing improperly fitted tennis shoes. And I know some young people who don't wear socks when they play tennis and wonder why they get blisters.

I suggest that when you buy a tennis shoe you try it on wearing one pair of thin cotton socks and over those a pair of heavy wool athletic socks. Then have someone check to be certain you have enough room between your toe and the toe of the shoe. Don't buy tennis shoes that are the same size as your regular street shoes and expect them to fit properly over heavy socks.

Is there any way to avoid cramps?

Cramps are often caused by tension. If I feel a cramp coming on during a match I try to stay relaxed because once a match starts, play is continuous unless it is stopped by the umpire. If a social player feels a cramp coming on, I recommend that he get off the court and take a warm bath, and that he treat the cramped area with hot towels. If the cramp persists it would be wise to call a doctor.

Do you recommend salt pills?

I believe that many players, including professionals, neglect to take enough salt tablets to replace the salt they have lost through perspiration. I know that when I forget to take my salt pills two or three hours before a match I often get a headache or cramps or feel extreme fatigue.

I can't recommend any particular dosage, however. It seems to vary with the individual. I remember that years ago I played a match against Ken Rosewall in Dallas on a boiling hot day. I had taken two or three pills before the match and it was so hot and I perspired so much that I had to take another four or five pills during the match. When I got into the locker room I found I had lost about eight pounds and was close to getting cramps. I asked a doctor if there was any harm in taking so many pills and his answer was that it didn't matter so long as it didn't upset the system. So I took two more and managed to avoid the cramps.

Normally, it is most beneficial to take salt pills a few hours before you play because it takes an hour or two for the salt to be absorbed into your system.

What about vitamins?

Have a checkup to determine whether you have any particular vitamin deficiency and then follow the doctor's instructions.

I know some players who believe in vitamins and organic diets. I know others who eat a lot and smoke and drink, but who play as well and seem just as healthy. If I get tired or hungry during a match I sometimes sip a glass of warm tea sweetened with honey because the body quickly turns honey into energy.

On the other hand I have always been so healthy that I never felt anything helped me as much as basic physical preparation and training.

Do you think it's a good idea to wear sunglasses when playing?

Speaking for myself, no. They seem to do something to my depth perception. But if a player has bad eyesight and needs to wear glasses, I see no reason for him not to wear prescription ground sunglasses with shatterproof lenses. Arthur Ashe wears glasses, and the only time he seems to be bothered by them is when it rains.

If you normally wear sunglasses and are going to play a match without them, I suggest you take them off at least half an hour before you play so your eyes can have time to adjust to the sunlight.

Warm-up

What is the purpose of the warm-up?

To loosen your muscles, get your strokes grooved, and begin to focus on the ball.

How should I dress for the warm-up?

As I grow older I find I have to dress more warmly. I usually wear a sweat suit, but if that doesn't appeal to you then wear a T-shirt under your tennis shirt; that will help you retain warmth and keep circulation going. When I feel I am ready to really start playing and I want the ball to behave properly, I switch to the type of attire I am going to wear during the match. I don't want to go out and try to groove a stroke and be restricted by a sweat shirt. So after I have warmed up, I take off my sweat suit and really start stroking the ball.

What is the proper way to warm up physically?

If you're running for a ball that's too wide you should never try to stop abruptly. Run yourself out in shorter steps and stop gradually. When you're not loosened up and you stop short, that's when you are going to pull a muscle. You should try and pick up momentum as quickly as you can but get into the fast tempo only when your match commences.

I suggest you hit deep because that means you are taking a full swing at the ball. Too many players aim the ball to just clear the net, ignoring the fact that such a ball usually falls 20 feet short of the baseline. So you should immediately assume a swing that aims the ball at the baseline.

You want to warm up with shots that you will be hitting most of the time, and these are the deeper shots. If you're on a very fast surface where you may be going to the net, you should be practicing your serve, your volley, and your angled placements for passing shots.

The slower the court, the more you should try for depth. Don't use the warm-up for short angle shots, which are used only when the rare moment of opportunity is there. Use your full strokes and don't neglect overheads, lobs, and volleys.

How much time is needed for a proper warm-up?

Most competitive players spend half an hour or more warming up prior to a match and, if possible, they play as much as an hour on the morning of their match. Once they set foot on the court for their match they are expected to be ready to go almost immediately.

The amount of time a social player needs to warm up varies with the individual and the time he has available on the court. If you have the court booked for only an hour and want to play two full sets, the warm-up must be brief. In that case I suggest you begin warming up before getting on the court, as I did during a period of my professional life when I played pro-sets, which were like sprints and had no warm-up time. If the spectators had come into the locker room before these matches they would have thought the players were crazy—we were always doing calisthenics, jumping up and down, and running in place thirty or forty minutes before we went out on the court. There was no time to loosen up or warm up once we began playing. We had to be ready and start fast.

If I am hurried before a warm-up, I usually hang loosely from the waist trying to stretch my muscles very very slowly. You'll find that as you do this you'll become more and more relaxed and will begin to drop toward your toes. I don't recommend active exercises such as knee bends which tend to bind you.

Can I do anything about the fact that I don't start to watch the ball closely for the first few minutes?

I've found the best way to correct this problem is to really concentrate hard on the ball from the first moment I get on the court. I repeat, concentrate on looking at the ball on all shots. I hit plenty of serves and overheads during the warm-up, forcing myself to keep my eyes on the ball.

Most people forget that in tennis as in golf they are required to focus and refocus on an object which is several feet away from them most of the time. We spend most of our day concentrating either on near or faraway objects, and a tennis ball is at an awkward distance for the eyes to begin to adjust properly.

If you win the toss do you choose to serve or do you select a side?

I'd rather receive than serve because I like to have the additional game to loosen up before I start to serve. Also, most players feel that because they serve first they have an advantage, but the truth is that they are at a psychological disadvantage; in many cases the server will lose the first point because of such overconfidence. Since the first game is usually the shakiest — even the top players don't have their rhythm set — I feel it's a good opportunity to try to break my opponent's serve. And in competition, where you change sides on odd games, when I come up to serve I don't want to be serving into the sun. If I take the sun on the first game, the next game will find me serving with the sun behind me.

On the other hand, if your opponent serves first and wins, it means that you will be serving to catch up, which may give him a psychological advantage. As long as he holds serve, you will always be serving from behind, and unless you have confidence in your serve, that may inflict extra pressure on you. I have a strong serve, however, and this situation doesn't faze me a bit.

You'll notice that many of the strong servers in pro tennis often choose to receive rather than serve, and that's because of the setup of the present

USLTA tie-breaker system of 9 points. At 6-all you're on even games, so the person who served first in the set serves first in the tie breaker. He serves two serves, then his opponent serves two, and then the first server has two more, taking care of 6 points. If the players are still in the tie breaker the person who chose to receive first at the start of the match has the last three serves. This is another reason I prefer to receive first.

2.
GROUND STROKES

Forehand

What is the correct forehand grip?

1. The butt of the racket should rest on the heel of your right hand.
2. Cradle the throat of the racket in your left hand.
3. Shake hands with the racket. Your fingers should wrap around the racket naturally and be slightly apart, not bunched together. The forefinger and the thumb should wind diagonally across the racket as in a handshake. Or, if you place your hand flat against the strings and then move it down the handle and grip it at the end, the correct positioning of the palm will come naturally.
4. Once you have the proper grip, hold the racket firmly and comfortably.

What is the first step in preparation for a forehand?

Turn your body sideways to the ball as early as possible. As you complete the turn your racket will automatically be in the middle of your body. From this position draw the racket back to its full ready position. You should then be able to hit any shot. Your knees should be bent, with the weight evenly distributed, your head down, and your eyes focused on the ball.

What is the fastest way to get the racket back?

The fastest way to get the racket back is to turn the body. This gets the racket started instantly. Obviously, if the racket is not back you have very little chance of making a shot, and there are many times when you will not be able to turn; but you should try to turn first, as I suggest. It will put you in a far better position all around to make a complete shot.

Should I take the racket back with a circular motion?

That is a waste of time and motion. It's much quicker to bring the racket straight back. The head of the racket may appear to have made a slight circular motion but the hand remains at waist level and the racket head is above wrist level. If the racket head dips it indicates that you have bent your wrist and are in a weak position.

What should I do with my left hand?

Most good players cradle the racket at the neck with their left hand, for two reasons: it takes some of the strain off the right hand and it can help snap the racket into position. There may be occasions when you don't have time to turn your body, so you use your left hand to help get the racket quickly into position.

SETTING UP FOR THE FOREHAND — Note racket going back with turn of the body, bent knees, and racket kept at midline of body until end of backswing

What is the proper height off the ground to hit the ball?

About waist high, or about 25 to 30 inches off the ground, just in front of your belt buckle. This is a fairly comfortable position in which to make contact with the ball, but since you have to get the ball over a 36-inch net, you must hit up and through it to carry it all the way to the baseline.

If you must back up a little to allow the ball to get to the proper height, try to move forward a little into the ball for power and rhythm, but only when you are actually hitting the ball.

When should I step forward into the shot?

When you get set. Step forward as you swing, transferring the weight from your rear foot to your forward foot.

How can I get more power into my ground strokes?

One way is through proper use of your wrist. By the time you get halfway through the stroke your wrist and hand start whipping the racket around much as in a serve. But the wrist is very sensitive and if you're at all tense you won't be able to control it, so I recommend most weekend players hit the ball with a firm wrist.

Another way to get more power (or to hit a heavy ball) is to keep the ball and the racket in contact as long as possible. Straighten your follow-through, keeping the ball on the racket a moment or two longer. This action is like increasing the length of a rifle barrel: the farther the bullet travels in the barrel, the more power it is likely to generate and the greater will be its accuracy. You must hit through the ball.

What should I be concentrating on as I am making a shot?

Concentrate on making your own shot, then evaluate and move accordingly.

How can I aim or direct the ball?

Reach out to the area you are hitting to with the head of the racket.

What is meant by hitting through the ball?

After the ball and racket make contact, the ball sinks into the racket strings and travels with the racket approximately 8 or 10 inches, and that is the period when you direct the ball or "hit through" it. The longer you hit through the ball the more power you generate and the more consistent your shots.

How can I keep from hitting the ball too far or too high?

You are aiming too high with the racket swing. Lower your sights.

How can I hit a top-spin forehand?

It's one of the hardest shots to hit properly because it takes a strong wrist action. In order to do it properly you must drop the head of the racket and then come up over the ball.

Where is the pocket of the racket?

About two strings below the true center of the racket.

What should I do after completing a shot?

Immediately return to the ready position in the center of the court.

Backhand

What is the correct backhand grip?

Cradle the throat of the racket in your left hand. The palm of your right hand should be on top of the racket when holding it parallel to the ground. The V between your thumb and forefinger is slightly to the left of the racket handle. The fingers should be slightly spread. Try not to bunch them together. I tend to keep my thumb up on the racket handle to help brace the racket at the moment of impact.

This is the same grip as the one you use on the service, volley, and overhead, except that in those cases the thumb is down around the racket.

How can I hit a backhand down the line?

If you want to hit down the line you have to make contact with the ball a trifle later and swing the racket head in that direction. A down-the-line shot should be the easiest shot you can make because you have a straight line to guide you.

How high should the racket head be at completion of a stroke?

Approximately at shoulder height if you have made a complete follow-through.

Should a backhand be hit in front of the right foot?

The backhand should be hit off your right hip. Advanced players hit it at a point a little farther forward.

HITTING A BACKHAND
DOWN THE LINE – Note late
contact with the ball

Why do most players tend to hit their backhand returns cross-court?

The main reason for this is that in hitting down the line from the backhand side you have 78 feet of court, but from the backhand side hitting cross-court you have an additional distance. It's a natural tendency when hitting through the ball to return it along the same line that it came to you.

Is it true that the backhand is the easiest stroke in tennis?

Yes. Because it's the most natural stroke. To execute the backhand you nearly always have to turn your body in order to get the racket back in the ready position, which means that more often than not you are hitting the backhand from a perfect stance, which develops consistency.

Also, right-handed players tend to focus with their right eye, so on the backhand they can focus with that eye. Also, when you stroke the ball, you should transfer your weight into the stroke. A right-handed player's right side is usually the stronger side, which means he is more comfortable leaning into the ball on his backhand. On the forehand you must transfer your weight to the left or weaker side, so you tend to do much of the work with your arm.

Most people are right-footed. A player taking off to his left or backhand side has a much quicker start because he pivots off his strong foot. Naturally, the reverse of all this is true for left-handers.

Why do many people take a backward instead of a forward step when they prepare to hit a backhand from the ready position?

This happens because some players are not quick enough to go forward, or they are afraid of the ball. In my own case, if I haven't been practicing for a while I will often start backing up into position instead of going into the backhand. Since I am aware that I am doing it, however, I begin to concentrate on taking a forward step with my right foot each time I go for a backhand. The more I practice this, the easier it becomes.

Is there a reason why most good players cradle the racket in their left hand in preparation for a backhand shot?

Just laying the throat of the racket lightly in the fingers of your left hand helps you in several ways: it takes some of the weight off your right hand, it helps you draw the racket back straight and close to your body, and it helps you snap back into position to hit a forehand. I also find that it gives me better balance when I am turned sideways and leaning into the ball.

PRACTICE TIP: Never neglect your strength. Many people who have good forehands go out and practice their backhand to the neglect of their best shot. Then they go out to play and find their backhand is working but the forehand is off because they didn't practice it. In my case, my backhand was my most consistent shot, but my fore-hand was my bread-and-butter shot, so I sometimes practiced six hours on my backhand and ten hours on my forehand. You should practice all of your strokes equally, but give a little more practice to your best shot. Make it even stronger—more dependable and more threatening.

Playing in the Backcourt

What should be my psychology when playing in the backcourt?

Always think aggressively. Your principal goal is to maneuver your opponent into a defensive position so you can move in and win the point.

You can't move in on every shot, but you should always have that in mind. Even if you have to back up to hit the ball you should be ready to move in and attack.

What is the best position in playing the back-court?

Your starting position should be about a foot behind the baseline near the center dividing line.

After hitting the ball from that position, however, your momentum will carry you 2 or 3 feet inside the baseline. You are then facing the net and your opponent and are subject to his next shot. If he manages to hit a shot deep to your baseline you must move back to recover and make your return. But if he hits a weak shot move in instantly.

Good players are constantly moving forward and back, always waiting for a chance to attack.

After what ground strokes should I not rush the net?

After very weak and short shots. Be patient.

Should my feet be planted on the ground when I make contact with the ball?

Your front foot should always be planted on the ground to help you pivot your body into and through the shot.

Should I always go to the net when my opponent has hit a short ball?

A player must go to the net when his opponent has hit a short ball. If the ball bounces high and short, you should be able to end the point then and there. Take your time, use a full stroke, step toward the net as you hit, and place the ball with accuracy. Think positive! If the ball is low, however, you must lift it over the net. This requires a soft shot but with enough depth to send the ball as close to your opponent's baseline as possible.

If the low, short ball comes to the forehand side, hit a forehand down the line and keep the shot low. Your opponent is then forced to hit a backhand passing shot. You should be waiting for it, favoring whichever side of the court the ball is on.

Which of my shots should I follow to the net?

A fairly good offensive shot, one that is deep and near your opponent's baseline so he has to step back to hit it or else take it on the half-volley.

Or, if you know that your opponent has a reasonably weak backhand or forehand and you have made him scramble to get a deep shot, that too is an ideal shot to follow to the net.

Is it safe to run to the net from the baseline after hitting a fairly deep shot to my opponent's baseline?

Not unless your shot has moved him back and out of position. Otherwise, he may catch you in no-man's land—the middle of the court about a yard back of the service line—and then you will be in trouble. Very few weekend players are quick enough on their feet to get to the net after a shot from their own baseline to their opponent's.

Why is it that I so often tend to overhit a ball when I am thinking in advance of going to the net?

Most players overhit under those circumstances because they have taken too long a swing when going to the net. You need just a short swing when rushing forward from inside the court.

Why is it that during a baseline rally I always seem to be the first one to hit a short shot?

Most players are not fully aware of how distant the baseline is. One bad habit which many players have is that of seeing the net as an immediate hazard, so it becomes their target. They think they are successful if their ball clears the net, so they don't swing at the ball hard enough. But the real target is the baseline.

In your case it's possible that after a few baseline exchanges you become cautious and tentative with your shots and stop hitting through the ball. As a result, your shots fall short. Try swinging a little more freely and aim for the baseline.

Is there any particular shot that is most dangerous to follow to the net?

Yes. A short shot which allows your opponent to get to the net first and puts him in a position to hit down at your feet.

In most cases, if you hit a ball short and in the center of your opponent's court and then rush the net you will be in trouble. You will find him in position to hit to any place in the court.

How can I get to the net against an opponent whose forte is putting away my angle shots?

That sounds like you're playing an incipient Rod Laver. When I competed against Laver I found that if I hit him a wide angle shot, I opened my entire court for him, but if I went to the center of the court I tended to confuse him.

What is the best percentage shot for me to hit from the baseline?

Keep the ball in play by trying to hit deep. Be patient! Wait for the right shot to become offensive.

How can I learn to make the short angle and soft shots the pros use?

It's a lot easier than you think.

I've had many people come to me and say they can't hit those shots, and then I've watched them play with their children and hit soft shots by the hour.

Imagine how gentle you would be if you were teaching a three- or four-year-old child to play tennis. Now, if you hit the ball with the same touch and follow-through that you would use with a child, your whole system will relax and you will suddenly become very gentle.

Use the same approach to finesse shots when you're at net. You'll be surprised how easy it is.

How can I hit a drop shot?

A drop shot is hit with a volley action. Your racket goes under the ball to develop the backspin needed to stop the ball.

When should I use a drop shot?

Use it when you are inside the service line and your opponent is on or behind his baseline. But don't use a drop shot too often. The value of this stroke is the element of surprise. The drop shot is very effective against a slow or tired opponent.

Never hit a drop shot when you are behind the baseline.

How should I follow up a drop shot?

If your opponent returns the drop shot, your parry is a lob. Your opponent will be running forward and will have to reverse himself.

After I have returned a ground stroke from behind the baseline where should I go next?

The more you can stay in the center of the court, the better off you are for any shot. Often when you watch a pro play, you probably say to yourself that he really gets to a lot of shots while not seeming to move much. What you fail to realize is that he is always returning to the middle section as fast as possible so he can cover the whole court.

Ground Strokes

If you hit a ball diagonally across court, you can cheat by staying a bit to the right or left of center.

I frequently start toward the net position but end up retreating. I know this is wrong but is there anything I can do to correct it?

You are probably chickenhearted and afraid to take a courageous swing at the ball, so you just tap it and allow your opponent to get to the net and crowd you back. What you must realize is that you are in a bad defensive position when you hit your opponent such a weak shot and are likely to lose the point anyway. Why not move in courageously and hit the ball like a hero instead of a coward?

When it's necessary to retreat, how far back should I go?

It is wise to go back far enough so that you have room to come forward after hitting the ball. Another thing: don't ever allow the ball to come to you. You should always go to the ball, not necessarily attacking it but always controlling it and not letting it control you.

Why is it that sometimes when my ground strokes are working well my serve seems to falter and vice versa?

That happens with all of us. Usually I found that the only time my game was completely together was when I was in perfect physical condition.

There may also be another reason. If you are serving well, the ball may not be coming back to you often enough to allow you to get into the groove with your ground strokes.

Sometimes you may mishit or blow a few easy strokes in the early part of a game and then lose confidence in those strokes. When that happens to me I will frequently run around the stroke and take it on the other side in order to get my confidence back, then gradually take more shots on the side that was not working well.

Concentration and hard work will usually bring back your stroke – that is, if you had it to start with. If not, learn to live with it, or continue practicing until you correct the problem.

PRACTICE TIP: You should take full advantage of every minute you are on the court and realize that every time you swing the racket it should be for a purpose.

When you pick up the ball after a point and want to hit it to your opponent, don't just flick at it without looking at it. Do something with the ball. Hit it right to your opponent so it bounces at the proper height; caress it so that it just clears the net; practice your backhand stroke. By making it a rule to do something special with the ball whenever you make contact, you will become more familiar with the action of the racket.

Always focus on the ball when you plan to hit it, even between points – otherwise you create a bad habit. By concentrating on the ball every minute you are on the court, you increase your overall ability to concentrate. Don't ever allow yourself to get sloppy.

What should I do if my opponent is on his service line after hitting a drop shot to me?

Usually you don't hit a drop shot in return. Your opponent is in so close that he will be on top of the ball too quickly, so get to the ball as fast as you can and hit to a corner.

What should I do if my opponent hits wide to my strength?

If you have a strong enough shot, go for the winner. You are out of court anyway. Most good players will play safe and lob, to give themselves time to recover for the next shot.

What is the cause of mishitting?

The basic cause of mishitting is your failure to focus on the ball. When you hit a good shot you are probably aware that you have focused on the ball very carefully, and when you think about a shot you have mishit, you probably realize you didn't see the ball clearly, if at all; it's important to realize that you can be looking at the ball but not focusing on it.

Almost every time a professional tennis player mishits the ball you can bet that it's because his view of it was distracted: his mind was elsewhere even though his eyes may have been on the ball.

The main thing that a coach in any ball sport will tell his players is: look at the ball. This is one thing tennis players should write all over their house. Focus on the ball. Focus on the ball.

If a normally good stroke has gone off during a game, what can I do to get it going again?

When a normally dependable stroke goes off, it's often because you are under pressure and have shortened your swing and started to play tentatively. Since you may probably be losing anyway, tell yourself that you are going to gamble on the next few points. Lengthen your swing and hit out, trying to send the ball to the service line. At the same time concentrate on watching the ball hit the center of the racket.

Even the pros have this problem, and often during a match a player who has just missed an easy shot will shout out, "Swing at the ball, idiot." And then on the next few points he blasts away at it and starts bringing the ball into the court again.

Being too tentative can hurt your good strokes.

BACKCOURT SUMMARY: Don't hit every ball to the obvious opening. Occasionally hit a ball to the spot your opponent is leaving. If you catch him on the wrong foot because he is going in the opposite direction, he will not be able to recover to reach the ball even though it is only 2 feet away.

Never move your weight back on any tennis stroke. If your weight is not transferred forward it will be difficult for you to generate any power.

Don't hit every ball the same way. Hit some balls harder than others and some higher or softer (but always deeper).

Keep your opponent off balance with the unexpected but do not try shots that are not in your repertoire.

Don't hit every ball to your opponent's weakness. When you get an opening hit a wide ball to his strength.

When you play against a better player, don't try to hit harder. Play your own game but try to be faster on your feet.

If a ball is hit deep to you hit it back deep. Your chance for a placement will come when your opponent hits short.

Watch your position on the court. Play several feet behind the baseline if your opponent is serving deep. Stand inside the baseline by several feet if he's serving short.

When your opponent is at net, hit low. When he's in the backcourt, clear the net by about 3 feet.

Hit harder when you are playing against the wind and hit softer when the wind is with you.

Cross-court is the basic ground stroke. On the forehand, keep your left side to the net and step in with your left foot as you hit. The moment of impact is one fraction of a second later if you are hitting down the line. When your cross-court and down-the-line shots are consistent and accurate, concentrate on properly transferring your weight, which will give you natural pace.

On the forehand, step toward the net with your

left foot just before making contact, using a hip–shoulder pivot to put all your weight behind the ball.

On the backhand, step in with your right foot, transferring your weight onto it as you make contact.

Almost every player is stronger on one side than the other. If your backhand is your weakness, play to the left of the center line. Just how far left you stand depends on your ability to cover the court and the pace with which your opponent hits. Play aggressively on your strong side. Never get tricked into overhitting on your weakness.

Footwork

The knees must always be flexed and the feet comfortably apart. Never stand stiff-legged. When running to the side, push off with the back foot—when running to the right, push off with the left foot; when running to the left, push off with the right foot. Don't stand flat-footed. Bounce lightly on your toes so you can be ready to push off quickly in any direction. Skip sideways to the ball when you have ample time. This automatically puts you on the proper foot after each move. If you have to pivot backward in order to get into position, try to take one step forward into the shot.

I notice that some players cover the court from
side to side with a side-stepping motion while
others just run for the ball. Is one method better
than the other?

Footwork is one of the most important facets of
proper tennis. A common fault of most weekend
players is to run directly toward the ball and then
prepare to hit it. They would be much wiser to
run to the side with the racket already extended,
so when they reach the ball all they need is a
short backswing and some forward motion to pull
the ball in.

When there is time, I prefer to use a side-stepping
motion, sort of like a boxer's shuffle. When I am
within reach of the ball I turn my body and stroke
the ball properly.

Can I improve my footwork?

Tennis is not a game of endurance. It's a sprinting contest and, with one or two exceptions, all
of the best tennis players have been very very
quick on their feet.

Ilie Nastase, for example, is not as fluid with
his strokes as some of the players he beats regu-
larly, but he is so fast on his feet that he is waiting for the ball most of the time regardless of
where it is hit. And if you are there waiting for
the ball you can hit it with a shovel and still get
it over the net.

I've had many players come to me and complain about their inability to improve their game.
I can usually help them in half an hour by taking

them out on the court and hitting balls at them harder and harder. After such a session they will be puffing, but I have made them move and consequently they realize they can move. A few hours later when they compete at their old tempo, the game will seem slow to them because of their footwork. The average person who wants to play better can improve a lot by speeding up his footwork.

PRACTICE TIP: To improve your footwork and sprinting ability, I suggest that after you have played a game you go out and jog as far as you can, then walk a bit and, when you have recovered, jog again, always expending a little more energy than you thought you had in you. Each day you do this you will improve your stamina.

This little exercise won't take you more than five or six minutes each day, but I maintain that it will improve your speed of foot so much that within a week you will be returning shots you would have considered unreachable.

Before starting this training program, it would be wise to have a medical checkup or ask your family doctor if he thinks you can handle the additional exercise.

3.
SERVING

What is the proper grip for serving?

The backhand grip, with the palm of the hand on the top of the handle. Almost every champion has used this grip for his service and overhead.

Why shouldn't I use my forehand grip for serving?

Because it prevents you from obtaining real power or the good spin control necessary to bring the ball curving into the service court.

Should I use the same grip for first and second serves?

You must use the same grip and the same approach for both serves so your opponent can't tell what kind of serve you are going to hit. At the last moment turn the racket head to the left to hit a flat serve, or angle the racket head and peel around the ball for a slice or top spin. This is what I call the "peeling-the-orange" motion—you wrap the racket around the ball as though the racket were a knife with which you planned to peel an orange, thereby producing the spin which curves the ball into the court.

What is the correct service action?

This can be best illustrated by an exercise I give to students. I usually take them out to a playground and give them an old racket. Then I walk about 200 feet away, mark a spot, and ask them to throw the racket that distance.

On the first few tries they'll usually be able to throw it only 25 or 30 feet because they don't realize how far they must extend their whole bodies and how high they must throw the racket to get the distance.

The proper service action is very similar to a throwing action.

Another approach I use is to ask a student to imagine that he has a hatchet in his hand and he wants to chop off a limb of a tree at the maximum height he can reach with the hatchet. I ask him to imagine that the racket is his hatchet and the ball is the limb.

You wouldn't just stab at a branch if you expected to cut it off. You'd take a good whack at it with all your strength, and that's what you must do with the racket and the ball at that last moment of the chain action of serving.

What is the proper toss?

If you don't think of the word "toss" but, instead, think of *placing* the ball over your head, you'll be well on the way to improving your serve. The ball is neither tossed nor thrown into the air; it is placed there. And that is one reason why, in my view, the serve is one of the easiest strokes in tennis. For all other strokes you must hit the ball wherever it comes to you, but when serving you have an opportunity to place the ball exactly where you want to hit it.

First, you should find your own height level by reaching up as high as you can with your racket in your right hand and stretching up on your toes. The distance from the ground to the top of the racket will probably be between 9 and 11 feet depending on your height.

The ball should be placed about 3 inches above your highest reach and you should strike the ball just as it starts its downward trajectory.

Now, take the ball in your left hand and drop the hand to your left side, holding the ball lightly with your fingertips. Stand in a reasonably comfortable crouched position and bring your left hand up from your side with a smooth, continuous action and extend the arm straight up. This extension of your arm and hand should be just fast enough to roll the ball out of your fingers and up in the air about 3 inches above the racket head. If the arm is extended without wrist action, the ball will go to almost the same height every time. The person who uses wrist action, however, will vary the placement; the ball will go either too high or too low. It must be a straight, simple motion.

PRACTICE TIP FOR SERVICE: A good way to practice proper ball placement for the serve is to find a room with a ceiling about 2 or 3 inches higher than you can reach with your racket extended. Stand in the room and practice placing the ball just under the ceiling. After you have released the

THE SERVICE TOSS — Holding
two balls, releasing off the
fingertips, starting the
swing, and extending

ball, let it drop to the ground. If your placement has been correct it will fall about a foot to the left of your left foot, if you're a right-hander. You can mark a spot in the area where it drops and then practice the placement. The ball should land within 6 inches of the spot each time.

Obviously no one, not even a pro, will place the ball in the exact spot every time, which means that when serving you may have to make a simple adjustment of your racket swing similar to the adjustment you have to make on every stroke.

Is there any difference in the placement on a windy day?

Yes. Instead of hitting the ball at the top of the placement you should try and make contact with it on its upward flight, while it still has a fairly straight movement. If you wait for the ball to go all the way up and hang in the air a moment, the wind may move it around.

Where should the racket head be directed when I am serving?

One of the biggest problems with serving is that most players don't realize they must swing the racket away from the target.

For example, when you swing the racket toward the ad court, the ball travels into the deuce court.

When you are serving, the racket starts off at an angle to the right in a kind of arc, but when the racket reaches the end of its arc it pulls the ball into the target.

THE SERVE — Note angle of racket head through later stages of swing ("peeling the orange")

Where does the power of a serve come from if the ball is not hit directly toward the target?

Power comes from snapping the wrist and turning the body into the serve just at the moment of contact. Many pros get additional power by also snapping the index and middle fingers in a chain reaction after the wrist snap. If you see one person who hits the ball at 90 mph and another who hits it at 100 mph, the difference is probably due to the fact that the fingers holding the racket gave that final burst of power as the racket made contact with the ball.

How are the fingers used?

Let's use the hatchet-and-limb example again. If you wanted to get more power into your swing with the ax you would use your wrist and fingers on the handle of the ax. just as you would use your wrist and fingers on the racket handle at the moment of contact.

The point at which you use your fingers is really a matter of timing. For instance, a person who throws a ball learns to use his fingers at the last moment before releasing the ball and he eventually learns how to throw farther by using his fingers for power.

What is the difference between the various types of serve?

The slice is produced by moving the racket face across the ball from left to right.

The American twist is imparted by moving the racket face from left to right and over the ball with a pronounced snap of the wrist. The racket comes around the ball as though it were a knife peeling an orange.

The flat serve is just what the name implies: the ball is hit flat without slice or twist.

What is the purpose of a slice or top-spin serve?

It will give you a safety factor because it clears the net higher than a flat serve before dropping into the service court.

You may also use a slice serve on a fast surface where the ball really skids and stays low. The slice will break to your left if you're a right-hander and to your right if you're a left-hander. On a very slick surface the slice serve will stay very low after it hits the ground and it will be more difficult for your opponent to handle.

I've heard it said that a player's serve is only as good as his second serve. What is meant by that?

That means if his second serve is good his overall service game is usually good.

Most weekend players don't have good second serves, however, which is why in my own instruction programs I so strongly emphasize the importance of a good second serve. If you don't get your second serve in you automatically lose the point. But if you can get a second serve into the court effectively you know you are going to get a play on your point, so practice your second serve more than your first.

My theory is that if a person knows he can get the second serve in he will be more relaxed and his percentage of good first serves will be higher.

Too often, weekend players tend to start hitting their hard first service too soon, before giving themselves a chance to get the range and to groove their strokes. It is probably better for you to build up speed and control gradually, rather than starting out with speed and too little control.

Where is the best place to stand for service?

When I am serving into the deuce court, I stand as close to the divider line as possible to give myself a larger target area to kick the ball into my opponent's backhand. When I serve into the backhand court, I generally move 2½ to 3 feet to the left of the divider line, which again gives me a better angle into the backhand.

Should I keep the same position for both serves?

When serving in a singles game it's fairly basic that the player stands more toward the center of the court, maybe a foot off to the right on the deuce court and perhaps 2 or 3 feet to the left on the ad court. If you're losing your serve, you might vary the position by standing a little farther to your right on the deuce court and serving wider, breaking the ball into your opponent. You can stand even more to the left when serving into the ad court and try to get a better angle into your opponent's backhand.

What should be my primary thought when serving?

You must always think of taking an offensive stand to win the point, especially on service. But first you must get the ball into the court.

Should you look at the place where you plan to aim the serve?

No, not directly, but you do kind of sight the service area in general, then make your decision, and commence your service action, making sure you are looking at the ball.

Where is the best place to aim a serve?

The best place is away from your opponent — to the corners. Occasionally you may want to be deceptive and catch him off guard by aiming directly into his body.

Should you decide where to aim the serve before starting the service action?

You should know where you are going to serve before starting your body movement, placement of the ball, and service action.

In most cases you should attempt to hit to your

opponent's backhand because a backhand return of serve is usually not hit as hard as a forehand return. If your opponent has a weak forehand, however, you may want to hit there more often.

What can I do if I have a weak serve?

Concentrate on getting the ball into the court and in play so that you can try to win the point with your other strokes, which may be stronger.

What is the object of the second serve?

The primary object is to get the ball into play so you don't end up throwing away the point. But with good practice you can still be offensive with your second serve.

I have seen some professionals who have had trouble serving and, believe it or not, they would serve underhand just to get the ball into play. During our recent tournament at Caesar's Palace, Cliff Richey served underhand against Brian Gottfried in the semifinals because Gottfried was intimidating him and because of a wind problem. Richey won a few points with his underhand serve, regained his confidence, and went back to his regular serve. However, Gottfried won the match with great tennis.

Serving

Should I always hit my second serve to my opponent's backhand?

That seems to be the standard approach, but I don't believe it is always proper. Everyone favors one side or the other. We are either right-eyed and right-footed or left-eyed and left-footed. Most people seem to have a quicker start to their backhand and can run faster to that side than to the other side because they pivot and start off on their strong foot.

My approach has always been to hit the second serve frequently to the forehand to keep my opponent off balance because he anticipates a serve to the backhand. Also, I know that he is more likely to be slower covering his forehand when he has to move off the weaker foot.

RULE OF THUMB: Vary your service more often to the forehand, even if the forehand is your opponent's strength. It keeps him off balance.

What if the receiver is moving over to cover for his backhand with a forehand return?

Concentrate on your own shot and you will overcome these tactics. You can also take a chance occasionally and hit a wide shot to his forehand to keep him in his place.

Should you swing at a second serve as hard as you do at a first serve?

I swing at the ball as hard, perhaps even harder, but the second serve has more spin or slice on it. The only way you can get either effect is by swinging fast, something most people fail to realize. They tend to let up and poop their second serve over the net, thinking that's the safest way to get it in.

The pro, however, relies on his slice or his spin for the safety factor, knowing his second serve will clear the net by as much as 3 feet and that the slice or spin will drop the ball into the court with a loss of some of its forward speed.

Why not use two first services?

For the crazy show-off, that's fine.

Do you suggest any special waiting period between a first and a second serve?

Everyone has a different rhythm, but I have found that when I served my worst it was usually at a time when my second serve followed the first too quickly. You should take your time with a second serve and give it as much care, preparation, and thought as you do the first. You'll frequently see some players bouncing the ball on the ground in front of them once or twice before a second serve. They do this deliberately to force themselves to take an extra moment and to get into the proper rhythm again. You also gauge the flight of the second serve by the flight of the first. Example: if your first serve hits the net you must raise your sights for the second serve.

What should I try to achieve with my first serve?

Consistency. Try to get your first serve in to keep your opponent from teeing off on the second serve. If your first serve is deep and has some speed, your opponent cannot get into an offensive position; he will remain tense and usually be standing somewhere around the baseline. But if you miss with your first serve, he will relax and move in about 4 or 5 feet and be in a more aggressive position and frame of mind. As server you generally have an advantage with your first serve, even if it lacks pace, so you should make the most of it.

Is there any purpose of the first serve besides attempting to win the point outright?

Yes. Most people don't realize the importance of the first serve as a guideline for what the second serve should be. If you miss with your first serve you should use it to determine the correction you will apply to your second serve.

To benefit most from a first serve you should try and visualize the angle and trajectory which the ball had and then plan the correction for the second serve. The person who thinks a little longer about the adjustment he will make on his second serve will probably do more with it.

What can I do if my serve is off?

Tell yourself to concentrate and focus on the ball, even more than you usually do. Force yourself to see the ball as you are hitting through it.

If your first serve is off, you should back off it and use only your second serve until you have built up confidence.

Again, that's why I think it's important for players at all levels to have a good, reliable second serve.

SUMMARY: Never rush yourself or allow your opponent to rush you.

The player who is trailing will too often hurry himself on the service.

Bounce the ball to get relaxed and comfortable after you have taken the service position. Serving before you are ready deprives you of concentration and this is the fastest way to lose the point.

Cut down on your power if your first serve is not going in at least 70 percent of the time.

Put your wrist, shoulder, and entire body weight into the serve every time you hit it.

Hit your second serve with a lot of spin, and swing *at* the ball.

Getting to the Net After Serving

Is it necessary to take a step or two toward the net after serving?

It's not necessary but it is advisable, if only to regain your balance.

If your serve has been properly executed the momentum of your body will automatically carry you those first couple of steps toward the net. This will, for the most part, help you regain balance and prepare for the next shot as well as put you in a position to cut off a weak return.

Must I go to the net after serving?

Going to the net is primarily an offensive tactic. If your serve was offensive then continue on the offensive. If your serve was soft go slower. But you should attempt to get to the net whenever possible after any stroke and take the offensive.

Should I follow a soft serve to the net?

It's not usually a good idea. If your serve is floating over the net and your opponent can really tee off on his return, it might be wiser to retreat to a couple of feet behind the baseline near the center of the court.

Is there any serve that is best to follow to the net?

Any serve that is aggressive enough so that your opponent cannot get set in time to do much with his return.

What is the best way to get to the net?

There is only one way to get to the net and that is as quickly as you can after evaluating your own serve.

How far into the court should I attempt to go after serving?

You should attempt to get as near to the service line as possible. If you can't make it there on any one shot then try to get there or even farther after your next shot.

Where should I aim the first volley?

You should generally aim any volley away from your opponent into open court.

What is the little jump pros sometimes make just before they stop running to the net after service?

That's not a jump, it's a straddle or ready position. The player has brought both feet together just as his opponent is preparing to hit the ball. After taking the straddle or ready position he is prepared to move in any direction for the next shot.

Why is it that so many of my running volleys either go out or into the net?

The fact that you are running for the ball indicates that your opponent has hit a good shot and put you in a defensive position, so you can expect to miss a greater percentage of these shots. The only way you can improve your running volley is to make an additional effort to get set more quickly and not be forced to hit the ball on a dead run.

What can I do if the ball bounces at my feet as I am coming in after a serve?

Try to get in a little faster so you can volley your return. If that's not possible, step back a few feet and hit the ball as a ground stroke or a half-volley deep to your opponent's baseline.

Is there any way I can compensate for the fact that I don't have the necessary strength or speed to get to the net after service?

You have probably accepted a habit that can be changed.

Spend a few practice sessions striving to get to the net after serving, trying to get closer to it each day. Continued practice will help you build up speed, stamina, and strength.

When should I retreat from the net?

When the ball has been lobbed over your head and you have to run back to get it. For the most part, however, it's never good to retreat from the net. Stand your ground. Your mere presence at the net is intimidating and puts pressure on your opponent.

PRACTICE TIP: Set aside some time with a friend for a practice session in which you serve, rush the net, and hit a volley. Ask your friend to return every serve he can, whether they land in or out, and then concentrate on getting to the net and volleying the ball in the center of your racket while continuing to move forward. A session or two of this will develop confidence in your ability to move forward and do something with a volley.

Return of Serve

Should I have a particular strategy in mind for return of serve?

My standard approach has always been to keep the service return low, forcing my opponent to dig up the ball. This limits his offensive and gives me a better opportunity to make an offensive second shot of my own. The basic idea of keeping the service return low is to make it difficult for your opponent to hit a winner.

If your opponent's serve puts you in an awkward position, however, it's enough just to get the ball back over the net and in play.

What is the best percentage shot for service return?

Keep your return low without trying to do too much with it. It's difficult for most players to volley a low ball or to hit it up, and a low return of service is especially hard to handle because the player either has to come in a long way to get the ball in the air, or else he has to step back and attempt a defensive half-volley — one of the most difficult shots in tennis. By returning the ball low and making your opponent move in, you can wear him down physically. But, if you can make an outright winner, then by all means do and forget about percentage play.

Assuming that I am waiting for a serve in the ready position, when should I turn to the side and start my racket back for the return?

The moment you see the ball come off your opponent's racket you should know whether it will be to your forehand or backhand, and that's when you should start your turn. Don't wait until the ball crosses the net. That's too late.

What if my opponent's serve to my forehand is weak?

Move into the ball and try to hit it as it is rising. Pound it at his feet or go for a winner.

What's the best way to handle a weak serve to my backhand?

Your forehand is probably your strongest shot, therefore you should run around a weak serve to your backhand and take it on your forehand. Continue to run around the serve, even if you miss the first few times; you are putting pressure on the server, who will begin to try to shave his margin of error more and more by hitting the ball deeper into your backhand. He will most likely end up making more service errors.

Isn't it embarrassing to run around a backhand?

No more embarrassing for you than it is for your opponent, whose serve is so slow or weak that you have time to run around it.

What you always want to do is take advantage of your strength and your opponent's weakness. That's a basic part of the game.

It may not be a normal movement for a person to run around his backhand to hit a forehand, because the footwork is almost like running backward, and it may be embarrassing to you if you don't do it well. However, the more you try it, the better you will become at it and the more offensive your game will be as a result.

Meanwhile you will be getting grooved with your forehand. The moment that an important point comes along, your opponent, who is serving, will probably say to himself, "He's running around my serve and hitting it with his forehand, so I'm now going to hit wide to his forehand and surprise him." Meanwhile you will say to yourself, "He knows I am going to run around his serve and hit forehands, because I've been doing it all along, so this time he'll probably try to surprise me by hitting wide to my forehand." So, you are putting pressure on him and forcing him to go for a winning serve, which may well result in a double fault.

The U.S. Davis Cup team used this tactic of running around the backhand serve to good effect against Australia in 1958 at Brisbane. Alex Olmedo had a good forehand but a weak backhand, and during his match the server was taking advantage of Alex's backhand. So in the rest period I told Alex that the moment the server placed the ball in the air he should move over and get ready to hit a forehand. This served two purposes: it got Alex into position to hit his strongest shot and his movement distracted the server.

What is the best way to handle a top-spin serve?

Cut it off at about shoulder level, hitting straight down and through the ball. Concentrate on hitting the ball in the center of your racket and aim for the server's feet; you have a better angle downward when you hit off the higher bounce of the top-spin serve.

How should I handle an extremely hard flat serve?

Basically you should catch the ball with a short punching, volley-type motion, taking advantage of your opponent's speed to give your own shot some pace. Hit through the ball, just trying to get it back over the net without attempting to do anything special with it.

If you have difficulty with the volley return, try standing back a little farther from the baseline so you can take a longer swing. If the ball consistently comes to the same place you may even want to take a chance and get your racket back very early to be prepared sooner and have a longer follow-through.

Or, you can just block the serve and return it as a lob. I saw this done most effectively some years ago at Forest Hills during a match between Rafael Osuna, the Mexican champion, and Frank Froehling. Froehling was not a great natural player, but he had a booming flat serve that scooted when it hit the ground. Because of this Rafael ended up standing about 10 feet behind the baseline to take Frank's serve. The question then facing Osuna was what to do with the serve. Froehling, who is over 6 feet, 4 inches, would rush the net and volley away Osuna's attempts at passing shots. There was only one thing Rafael could do. He just stood behind the baseline and threw up high lobs. The spectators, some of the other tennis players, and the newsmen were sitting on the sidelines saying, "What the hell kind of tennis is this in the finals at Forest Hills?" But I agreed with Rafael. The idea of the game is to win and to use whatever tactics are necessary to achieve this end without being unfair. Rafael found that the high lob worked, so he used it. I admired him for being able to analyze the problem, develop a counterattack, and stay with it. Eventually he won the match and the U.S. Championship.

My point is, you should use any kind of tactic you can to get the ball back to the server.

As a right-hander playing a lefty, how can I expect his serve to bounce?

The ball will always bounce in the opposite direction of a right-hander's serve.

When a left-handed opponent serves to your backhand in the ad court, the ball will usually move away from your backhand. When he serves a slice to your forehand, the ball will tend to crowd into your body. A top-spin serve will kick out away from your body.

How can I handle a lefty's serves?

The best way is to play against left-handers more often and familiarize yourself with their serves.

When I play against a left-hander I generally

take an offensive position on his serve and step in closer so I can cut it off before the spin takes over.

If my system doesn't work for you, then step back about a yard or so behind the baseline, wait for the spin to wear off, and then return the serve as a normal stroke.

If you know in advance that you are going to play against a lefty, seek out a left-handed player and practice with him. Work on your backhand return — the serve will generally come to that side.

What if my opponent does not come to the net after serving?

If your opponent stays back, simply hit your return deep to his weakness. And try to take an offensive position by moving in.

How should I defend against an opponent who rushes the net after serving?

Try to hit past him. Keep the ball low and make him volley. If that fails and he keeps crowding the net push him back with a lob. When he becomes aware that you're going to use an occasional lob, he won't come in so close and a passing shot will be more effective.

The best way to learn how to handle net rushers, however, is to play against them often. When they are good, they are very difficult to beat because they are always putting on the pressure.

What can I do if my opponent is quick-serving me?

Courtesy dictates that your opponent must give you time enough to get set, and every player has the right to put his hand up and stop play if he feels he has been quick-served. Nothing will break your opponent's rhythm more, and he will soon allow more time between his serves.

Are there any legitimate tactics I can use to upset a server?

Don't stand in the same place each time you receive service. You should try as many receiving positions as you can to determine which one will put you in the best position to take advantage of the serves.

Although Ilie Nastase is often criticized because he stamps his feet just before an opponent hits a shot, or moves when his opponent is about to serve, the fact is that his tactics are legitimate—they are designed to win points rather than make friends. Anything you do, short of throwing a racket at a player, is permissible, although not necessarily acceptable. The rule books are mute on this point.

If your opponent is concentrating fully on his serves, nothing you can do will upset him, and vice versa.

SUMMARY: Watch the ball come off your opponent's racket.

Keep your knees flexed and your legs a comfortable 10 to 14 inches apart.

Start your backswing early so that you can meet the ball rather than have the ball meet you.

Bend your knees. Try to step in toward the net as you hit.

Stay down to the ball with knees flexed throughout the return. Don't straighten up until the end of the follow-through.

When the follow-through is completed, hop or slide into position immediately so you can be ready for the next shot.

If your opponent comes to net constantly, throw up a few high lobs over his backhand side. This will keep him from coming in too close and your passing shots will then be more effective.

Take a shorter swing on hard first serves and be very alert.

4.
NET PLAY

What grip should I use at net?

Most players have found that the Continental or backhand grip is best for net play. One advantage is that you can hit a forehand volley at a later point in front of you or behind you just by turning your hand up and forward. The same shot would be difficult to handle using the forehand grip.

If you use the Continental grip, however, you should lower your body more. In fact, it is a good rule of thumb to crouch lower and lower as you approach the net.

What is the most important thing to remember at net?

To be aggressive — to try to put the ball away.

What distance should I stand from the net?

There is no set distance, but I feel that the ideal starting position is about 12 feet from the net or almost halfway into the service box. If you are too close you are vulnerable to a lob, and if you are too far back it will be difficult to make effective volleys.

If your opponent hits a ball that is just going to drop over the net, you should go forward instead of waiting for the ball to come to you. If you move toward the net you have a better chance for an angle shot or placement.

I usually move in as close as possible to the net because the closer I am the better opportunity I have to get to the ball quickly and clear the net with my shot. It's also apparent that my proximity to the net is a threat to my opponent, thereby putting pressure on him to make a good shot.

When should I play offensively at the net?

Always. Hit away from your opponent, and if you are unable to angle the ball, keep it deep and in the court rather than attempt a very low percentage shot. It doesn't take much hand movement to angle a ball, although for the average weekend player it does take a lot more practice.

How can I anticipate the direction of a ball hit from the baseline when I am at net?

Experience helps you anticipate, of course. But if you don't have much experience you should watch your opponent carefully until he has completed his stroke and you should balance yourself according to his movements. If he moves as though he is going to hit cross-court you want to balance in that direction. You're not guessing; you're analyzing where he is going to hit the ball by the way he holds his racket, the positioning of his feet, and what you have already learned about his likes, dislikes, and capabilities.

The Volley

What should I do if I don't have a good volley?

Go out and practice it more. Concentrate on hitting the ball in front of you and in the center of the racket.

If you are in a game and your volley is off you should favor your ground strokes and stay at the baseline. Occasionally you should still try to bluff your way to the net, if for no other reason than to intimidate your opponent and maybe put a volley away.

What kind of action should I use for volleying?

Most players use very little action in dumping an angle shot but you should actually punch under and around the ball to make an angled volley. I play extremely close to the net except when coming in after service for the first volley. From the net I try mostly for angle shots and only volley deep on the first ball when caught behind the service line or when the ball is very low.

The wrist is always laid back and firm. The wrist action is directed toward the ball away from the body for the volley.

Should I hit down on a volley or swing level?

You should punch down on the volley when it is high because you are usually hitting down into the court. Never swing level at a volley and never take long strokes at the ball when you are at net, because in all probability by the time you get the racket back the ball will have gone past you. When at net you should try to hit the ball in front of you where you can see it best, using a very short punching stroke. Keep the ball on the racket for at least 6 to 8 inches.

Why do I so often hit a volley past the baseline?

Probably because you have taken too long a stroke. You must firm up your wrist and use a short punching stroke.

Why do I frequently get nailed at the net by a ball hit directly to me?

Because your opponent has hit a good shot! It is possible that your racket may be a little too heavy for you to move it around quickly at net so you may want to try a lighter racket. The backhand position, with the racket just at your belt buckle, will usually handle most shots, but remember to keep the wrist firm.

What can I do if a ball is hit directly at my face?

At all times keep your eyes on the ball and if it should be hit at your face, all you have to do is move 3 inches to one side or the other, or just duck your head. Don't close your eyes! That's the worst thing you can do.

THE VOLLEY—Hitting a low return, and a high return off forehand and backhand; note short punching stroke and downward angle on the high returns

If the ball hits you, the worst that can happen is that it will sting about as much as a light slap.

Why is it that I frequently catch a volley behind me?

You are probably in the habit of taking the racket back too far, which keeps you from bringing it into the hitting area quickly enough.

You should try to catch the ball in front of you, using a shorter backswing.

Where is the best place to aim a volley when my opponent is also at net?

At his feet, so he cannot make an offensive shot. The next most vulnerable spot for any player is just above the right hip because it is difficult to get the racket there quickly.

Try for winners only when you are certain of making them. Otherwise play the percentages.

What should I do if I have hit a really short lob and am at the net when my opponent moves in to clobber it?

You should take what we refer to as the "matador stance." Immediately turn sideways to your opponent, keeping your eyes on him and your racket held firmly behind your body in a ready position. The ball may be hit somewhere near your racket, giving you a chance to make a shot, while at the same time you have presented the smallest possible target for your opponent.

If I am already at the net when should I move in even closer?

When the ball has been hit weakly. But don't move in too close to the net prematurely, and never move until you have seen your opponent hit the ball. You should set yourself in a balanced position ready to move in any direction, but don't crowd the net because he will then throw up a lob. If he hits a weak shot move in as close to the net as possible and put the ball away.

Why do I often fluff the easy setup shots at the net?

For the same reason that a pro golfer sometimes misses a 2-foot putt: lack of concentration. As good a player as I was, I learned very early to have respect for the easiest shots because the moment you get overconfident, or think you've won the point before you've hit the ball, that's when you are most likely to miss.

When you have an easy setup shot you must concentrate even harder to make certain you are looking at the ball, not at your opponent. Watch the ball constantly until you have completed your shot.

How should I handle a ball which is coming low over the net and dropping?

Do not dip the racket head. Instead, drop your hand, keeping your wrist firm and the racket head on a level with or above your hand. Lower your body by bending at the knees and try to keep your eye level down to the flight of the ball to help yourself sight the shot.

Hit the ball deep into the court. After you have evaluated your return, try to get into position to cut off the next shot and win the point.

Should I try to hit angled volleys?

Of course, but realize that this is a difficult shot. Your purpose at net is to be aggressive and win the point whether it calls for an angle or deep shot.

How and when should I hit a half-volley?

A half-volley is used when you're on top of the ball immediately after it bounces in the middle of the court. It is an extremely difficult touch shot because you just pick the ball up and float it back to the baseline.

To make the shot, take your racket down almost to the ground and, as the ball bounces and starts to rise, come up and forward with the racket. What you're doing is actually picking the ball up immediately after it bounces. Don't swing or hit at the ball. Just push it forward.

How and when should I hit a lob volley?

A lob volley is used when your opponent is also at net and has hit a volley which you are unable to do much with, and you want to push him back to his baseline. You should angle your racket head under the ball and, using a punching wrist action, lift the ball up over your opponent's head. This is a difficult shot to make, and if it is not executed perfectly you are vulnerable.

How and when should I hit a drop volley?

The drop volley is a difficult do-or-die shot made when you are in an aggressive position at the net and your opponent is around his baseline. Drop your racket head just under the ball using a quick wrist action to get around and under the ball, as if you were peeling an orange. Then drop the ball over the net so that it falls short in the court.

How should I handle my opponent's half-volley and drop volley?

You want to be able to read the movement of his racket as quickly as possible so you can balance and prepare for the shot.

If your opponent hits a half-volley to you, you should be able to hit it wherever you want using a solid ground stroke.

If the lob volley is over your head you must start running backward to get it. If it is within reach of your overhead drive it right down into the middle of the court.

When you suspect that a drop volley is coming off your opponent's racket, start running in the direction you think the ball will most likely go. Move the moment his racket head goes under the ball. You want to get a fast start on the shot if possible.

How do I make a backhand half-volley?

Take the racket back with your left hand and get down as low as possible to the ball with your left knee close to the ground. Step toward the net with your right foot and hit the ball well in front of you. Catch the ball just after the bounce.

Where is the best place for me to return a volley?

Away from your opponent.

Even the better players realize the best they can usually do with a low volley is to simply return it deep. If you hit the ball deep enough in the court you will keep your opponent back and force him into a defensive position.

PRACTICE TIP: To strengthen reflexes and hand and eye movement at the net, pros frequently have practice and training sessions in which one player stands at the net while two others stay on the baseline and rifle balls at the net man until his arm is ready to fall off. The net man will very quickly get in the habit of catching the ball out in front of him and he will soon be able to anticipate where most of the balls will be hit.

The Overhead

What is the action for the overhead?

It is truly a punch stroke, more of a forceful swing than anything else, but you must swing straight through the ball. Again, use the example of a hatchet cutting a branch as your guide.

Do I use the same action for an overhead as for a serve?

The action is almost the same but the swing for an overhead is not quite as long.

For an overhead you should have the racket behind your back in its most comfortable position, as though you were going to throw it to the end of the court. I like to think of the racket behind the back as being almost like the trigger of a gun. Your head should be up and your eyes focused on the ball. When the ball is a few feet over your head, start your swing forward or, literally, pull the trigger.

Should I use my left hand to point at the ball when I am hitting an overhead?

Some players do, but I prefer to leave my hand comfortably out of the way.

Should I always try to smash an overhead?

Placement on overheads is far more important than pace.

You should play an overhead to win the point because it's the one shot where you are inside the court and hitting down on the ball from a set position with plenty of time to get ready.

Your thinking should be aggressive and, for the most part, you should attempt to hit a winner, which usually means into the open court. If you see your opponent starting to move into that area, however, smash the ball behind him.

Should I hit an overhead as hard as I would a serve?

Yes and no. If you are catching the ball in the air before it bounces, it is coming down at a faster pace than it would from your service placement and you can swing at half the speed you would use on a serve and still get a lot of speed on the ball.

At the same time, if the ball has bounced it has very little pace as it comes down, and you should make up some of the speed with your swing.

Even after the ball bounces I have difficulty judging it. What can I do about that?

If you were playing outfield in a baseball game and the batter hit a high ball, you would stay back, wait, and judge the ball's flight, and then as you moved in to catch it you would have your glove right in front of your eyes so you could watch the ball.

You do exactly the same thing when a tennis ball is coming down from either a lob or a high bounce. Stay back and keep your eyes on the ball, making last-minute corrections as you move under the ball. When the ball is dropping in front of you, hit up into the flight of the ball, catching it in the center of your racket, and then hook it down into the court as you would with a serve.

You may find that at the beginning you will hit a lot of overheads toward the fence, but as you start to get the range you'll begin to hook the ball down into the court.

Is there any particular place I should attempt to aim an overhead smash?

As with every stroke, you want to hit away from your opponent and into the open court. Again, psychology plays a part. If your opponent is in the center of the court and knows you are going to hit an overhead smash, he generally anticipates that you will hit it to one corner or the other. In this case, it might be a good move to hit the ball right at him.

It's also good psychology to hit to your opponent's forehand from time to time because most people don't seem able to move as quickly to the right as to the left.

Why do players often tend to hit overhead smashes into the net?

This happens because the racket head is coming down on a ball that is also dropping. The racket head should actually be coming up into the ball. Remember the ball stays on the racket for a distance of 8 or 10 inches, so as you come up under the ball and hit through it your wrist action hooks the ball down into the court.

What is the trick to running backward and jumping for an overhead smash?

That's no trick; it's practice and usually only a pro can do it. You will probably notice that pros use a lot of wrist movement to bring the ball down into the court.

PRACTICE TIP: To hit the overhead smash off a bouncing lob, have someone hit high lobs to you while you are standing behind the baseline. Let the lobs bounce first. Have your racket back in the ready position, behind your back, and then try to hit up and through the ball.
Try to catch the ball in the center of the racket, slightly in front of you, hitting up and through it

with sufficient elevation and power to send the ball to the fence on the far side.

After practicing this for some time, begin to use your wrist to bring the ball down into the court.

The Lob

What is a lob?

A lob is a controlled ground stroke in which you open the face of your racket. The trajectory of a lob is high, the idea being to lift the ball high and deep into your opponent's court.

Do you consider the lob kind of a sissy or weak stroke?

I'm glad you smiled when you asked that question.

I doubt that you would call me or some of the other top pros sissies or weak, but we all use lobs effectively and offensively.

The lob is an underrated shot. It's even more important for the weekend player to take advantage of the lob because most of his opponents are not likely to have good overheads.

For the most part the lob can be a very offensive shot, and I strongly recommend that players of all levels learn to hit lobs and, conversely, overheads.

What is the difference between an offensive and a defensive lob?

An offensive lob is used to win the point. A defensive lob is used to gain time to recover.

When should I use an offensive lob?

The offensive lob can be hit when you are in a position for a ground stroke or a passing shot.

What is the proper stroke for an offensive lob?

You should try to delay your shot by faking a short ground stroke, so your opponent leans toward the net. At that precise moment you should take a smooth swing, hitting through and over the ball so that it climbs literally straight up until it loses its forward momentum and drops quickly into the court.

The offensive lob is popular with some of today's tournament players, but it's a difficult shot and the average player who uses it will have to practice it quite a bit.

When should I use a defensive lob?

A defensive lob is usually hit from behind the baseline or from an out-of-court position to allow yourself time to get back onto the court.

If a point is important and you are behind the baseline, you may throw up a high lob to let your opponent know the pressure of the point is on him.

During a fast-paced point you can lob to upset your opponent's rhythm and give yourself time to gather strength.

A series of defensive lobs will help wear down an opponent in good condition, especially if you are lobbing with the sun behind you.

What is the proper stroke for a defensive lob?

Draw your racket back and take a full swing at the ball with a firm wrist. Do not flick at the ball, any more than you would on any other shot. It's the follow-through of your racket that gives the lob its distance.

As with every shot in tennis, but especially with a lob, it's most important you keep your eyes focused on the ball.

How can I hit a top-spin lob?

Drop the racket head below the flight of the ball and hit up and over the ball with the same movement you would use if you were going to peel the ball like an orange. Use the same movement on your backhand and forehand, but remember that this is a very difficult shot to hit.

Should a top-spin lob be hit down the line or cross-court?

Almost every shot should be hit away from your opponent. The top-spin lob is no exception, but the shot is hard enough to control without being too concerned about precise placement; it's enough to just hit it to the deepest part of the court.

What is the best way to handle a top-spin lob?

It's usually better to catch it in the air before it bounces. A bounce off a top-spin lob will run away from you quickly and is very difficult to catch.

What is the best way to handle a high lob?

If the lob is coming down from a height of 30 to 50 feet, it will be dropping quickly and its speed will be difficult to judge. If you let the ball bounce it may only go up 20 feet and when it comes down the second time it will be dropping slower, giving you more time to judge its speed and to hit it in the center of the racket.

Where should I aim a lob?

Close to your opponent's baseline. The highest spot in the lob's trajectory is roughly over the net, midway in the flight of the ball.

Are there any lobs which I should follow to the net?

A high lob that lands inside your opponent's baseline and bounces high might be good to follow to the net, depending to a large extent on your opponent's overhead. If his overhead is weak, you should get to the net quickly to close the court off and thus turn a defensive shot into an offensive move. If your opponent has a good overhead, stay back behind your baseline because he will probably smash the ball down your throat.

What is the best strategy to defeat a lobber?

The answer to the lob is the overhead smash. If you keep blasting winners off your opponent's lobs he will soon be forced to play another shot.

Failing that, you must have the same type of patience and attitude that your opponent has. Don't give him any indication that his lob bothers you.

Remember that lobbers are usually not very good at net, so a smart approach is to draw your opponent up to the net, then either lob over him or try for a passing shot. And you can try to run him so he doesn't have time to get into position to make his favorite shot.

It is not fun to play against a consistent lobber, because a lobbing game is frequently a question of patience. Either find an answer for the lobber or don't play against him, but if you avoid him you are only defeating yourself by not accepting his challenge.

If you show your disgust toward someone who lobs, they'll continue lobbing if they really want to win the game. So you must use the approach that their lob doesn't bother you and even give them credit, although you may have to smile through clenched teeth. This is where psychology enters into it.

Why is it that I frequently lob short?

You probably don't realize that the baseline is some distance away and you may make your opponent the target rather than the baseline.

5.
PSYCHOLOGY
AND
STRATEGY

What is meant by playing percentages?

Don't go for the big shot when you don't need it!

It's unfortunate that we don't keep tennis records as they do in baseball, noting the errors made by players. If we did, you would probably be shocked at the number of matches that have been won not on winning shots but on the errors of the losing player.

Rod Laver is one of the few players today who can win matches by hitting outright winners, but when he loses matches it's because he allows himself very little margin of safety. He plays every shot for a winner and when he's on, he's great, but when he's off, he's terrible.

Actually, all the colorful big hitters have been like this, while the percentage players have always been less interesting to watch. A percentage player like Frank Parker never created much excitement, yet even today, in his fifties, he wins exactly the way he won when he competed professionally—through the errors of his opponents.

How should I play percentages?

Play it safe and let your opponent make the errors.

Can you give me some examples of percentage play?

Let's say you have been drawn wide off the court and have the opportunity to make a sensational passing shot. Percentagewise you will win more points by throwing up a high defensive lob. It gives you an opportunity to get back onto the court and it puts your opponent under the pressure of having to make an overhead and a possible error. The sensational passing shot is a low percentage play, especially if your opponent is in a spot to cut it off.

Percentage tennis also applies when the court is wide open, when your opponent has left the court or has fallen. Under such circumstances some players try to hit a better than average shot when a dink shot would be good enough. Don't go for the big shot when you don't need it. That's the sum of percentage playing.

Do you watch your opponent when playing?

No. I try to be respectful and even cordial when he makes a good shot, but the more important the match, the less attention I pay to the player on the other side of the net.

My total concentration is on the ball and what I intend to do with it. I may sense that someone has hit the ball to me, but I know that the moment I give my opponent an identity or sneak a peek at him, I have lost my concentration.

I believe the only way to make a good shot is to

concentrate on every point with your mind clear and focused totally on hitting the ball and completing your stroke. This way you will make a better shot and you will force your opponent into making the next shot, thus turning the pressure on him.

If you are in a good position for a forehand down the line, then your total concentration should be on that shot, even if you sense your opponent may cover for it.

Do you work out your strategy before a game?

I have the feeling that most weekend players do not pay much attention to their opponent's weaknesses and strengths, even though they may play against that person often. Every player has weaknesses and you should practice the shots that will capitalize on these weaknesses. If your opponent tries to improve his shots in the meantime there will be even more of a challenge involved, and that also is part of the strategy of playing.

How can I determine my strategy during a game?

During the early part of a match you will find out which of your shots make your opponent most uncomfortable and which shots are his weakest ones. You should develop your strategy based on his weaknesses and your strengths. Never neglect your strengths. The shot that disturbs him the most is the one you want to hit to him most often, just as the thing he does best is what you want to avoid letting him do.

It's often a good idea, however, to use a surprise attack to his strength, particularly if you have been playing his weakness for some time. Mix up your shots enough to keep him off balance and stop him from getting grooved with one particular shot. And if you lose a game, accept it. But, generally speaking, you still must play your opponent's weaknesses.

If he has a weak serve, try to run around it and hit your strongest shot off it, thus putting yourself in an offensive position and putting pressure on him to do more with his serve.

You should know your opponent's age and physical condition. If you know that someone is out of shape and short on endurance, you might plan to play the first set in a more relaxed manner, not worrying so much about winning points as making him run a lot and fight for every point. An approach of that type on the first set will help you groove your own shots because you won't be trying for winners; you will just be trying to keep the ball in play and wear him down. But you must still keep in mind that you are trying to win the set.

What strategy should a man use playing against a woman?

Most women are very vulnerable to a drop shot or a lob, whereas in men's tennis you must hit both of those shots nearly perfectly or you will lose the point. These shots can be used most effectively against women, as Bobby Riggs proved in his celebrated match with Margaret Court.

There's no way a young woman can compete physically against a young man, and I think that should be an accepted fact. A good male player can almost always beat a good female player because he is faster and has more stamina and strength.

I have practiced with many of the women players on tours, and they hit a lot of balls back and we have a lot of fun. But if men were to play competitively against women the handicap we would have to give them in tennis, or most any other sport, would be frightening.

How can I improve my anticipation?

This can be done only by playing a lot of tennis and analyzing a lot of players.

An experienced player is like a computer programmed with every item of information available (to him): his opponent's speed, likes, dislikes, capabilities, and incapabilities. At the moment his opponent strikes the ball, even more information is fed in — the movement and flight of the ball, its speed, the angle of the shot, and the speed of his opponent's footwork. All these items enable the experienced player to make a quick analysis, to anticipate, and he moves or balances to where he expects the ball to be hit.

Anticipation is not guesswork, however. It's analysis. One way for the average player to sharpen his anticipation is to watch his opponent's feet, body, and racket. Have an awareness of the likelihood of his making certain shots from certain areas of the court. For example, if you have hit a cross-court, the shortest distance for his return is down the line; read the motion of his body and position as he comes around the ball. Any move on his part which gives you an idea of where the ball is going should be analyzed before he hits the ball. Then you balance yourself in the direction where you believe the ball is going and you move the moment the ball has been hit.

If your opponent happens to hit the ball in a direction other than the one you anticipated then give credit where it's due.

REMINDER: After each shot try to go back to the center of the court as quickly as possible. You will usually have less distance to move on your opponent's next return.

Should I look at my opponent just before hitting the ball?

Never look directly at your opponent because the moment he can see your face or eyes he has been given some indication of where you may hit the ball.

You should always be aware of his location on the court without ever really looking at him. An advanced player is like a calculating machine. For example, I know that a ball will take half a second to travel from my opponent's racket to a position on my side of the court, and that it will take him a second and a half to recover to where I'm going to return it, so I have a one-second lead on him if I hit the ball properly.

Which are the most important points in a game?

The hardest points to win are usually the most important: service break, set point, and match point. These are the hardest because an opponent with his back up against the wall will usually fight harder and concentrate more on these than on the previous points.

You probably know this from your own game and realize that if you played each point as hard as you play match point when you are down, you probably wouldn't ever be down.

Do you believe in playing all points hard?

Yes, assuming you have the physical stamina to do so and are not pacing yourself. By playing all points hard you will get more out of your game and psychologically you will also eliminate the letdowns that occur from time to time.

Do you suggest planning one shot ahead?

Occasionally, but for the most part you should concentrate fully on hitting your shot into the open court—everything happens so quickly in a game it's hard to plan in advance.

113

Should I vary my game according to the score?

Yes, particularly if you are an older player. If you're down 30-love you may not want to burn yourself out trying to make up the difference, unless you think your opponent is a little more tired than you are, in which case try to run him a little farther to wear him down.

If you're down 40-30 on your serve, make certain your first serve goes in so your opponent has to fight for the point. This is a vital point in the game and may make a difference between winning or losing a set.

If you're far behind in a set and you have another to play, there's no point in wearing yourself out unless you think your opponent is also tired. Save yourself for the next set.

Should I make adjustments in strategy if I am losing?

Do anything you can to get back on top but, for the most part, stay with your strength. And never switch to a game you don't know how to play. If you are basically a baseline player, don't become a net rusher after losing a set. Try a change of pace, such as more lobs or softer shots, or switch from playing your opponent's backhand and play his forehand.

What is meant by "never change a winning game"?

If you are winning by playing from the baseline don't start coming to the net. If you are winning by coming in on every service don't start staying back. Whatever you are doing, it is right, so there's no reason to change it.

What if you don't feel like playing, but you must?

I've been in that boat very often and it's tough, but I've had to play. Sometimes when I feel that way before a match, I splash ice water on my face and rub some on my legs and forearms to get the blood moving and tingling. Then, when I get out on the court, the adrenaline starts to flow and the desire to win returns. Oddly, I've played some of my best tennis when I felt the least like playing. I kept saying to myself, "Run. Watch the ball. Concentrate." And in time I found my groove and got into the game.

Professional and tournament players are often exhausted before and during games they must play. Most of them know, however, that if they are tired from the strain of previous games, their opponent is probably equally tired. So they try to fake it and bluff their way through. They will act calm and pretend they have energy by jumping up and down and smiling from time to time as though they aren't under pressure. This serves two purposes: like actors playing a role, they will sometimes get carried away and actually believe they have energy; and their opponent will believe it too.

Occasionally, it's a good idea to accept the fact that you're tired and say to yourself, "I'm likely to lose this game so I might as well relax and just hit out." Most players will be surprised at how well and hard they can hit a ball if they are relaxed. After you've made some good shots, chances are you will get into the spirit of the game.

Is there any way I can help rid myself of tension during a game?

Yes. There are normally two types of tension during a game: mental and physical. I don't know of any player who hasn't been troubled by one or both types at some time or other.

You will frequently see pros like Ken Rosewall or Rod Laver sort of hang loose or squat between points trying to relax their systems.

I make it a practice to relax my body between points and tense up only when I go to make a shot. I've found that the more I relax, the better I usually play, and the better I play, the more I feel like playing, thus creating a beneficial cycle.

I know many players who, to relax their nerves, take a deep breath through the nose and at the moment they make contact with the ball they exhale through the mouth with a whoosh. They claim this not only helps them relax but helps clear their lungs and gives them an extra burst of energy. Inhaling deeply through the nose and exhaling through the mouth several times should help anyone relax a bit.

Relaxing mentally is really a question of mind

over matter. When you feel yourself tensing up, tell yourself to slow down, concentrate on the game, and focus your eyes on the ball. Tell yourself that it's not important that you win, it's only a game. That's what I tell my students, but in a match it's sometimes difficult for me to practice what I preach.

Another way to overcome tension is to make up your mind to attack, to run. The harder you run, the looser your body will get and the more naturally you will be able to perform.

How can I keep from getting sloppy during a match?

When you find yourself getting careless, you must concentrate harder, even replay some of the previous points in your mind. A good tennis player is like a good poker player: he can remember every move he or his opponent has made. Chances are you will realize that you didn't see the ball clearly the last few times you hit it. So you must say to yourself over and over like a broken record, "Focus on the ball."

If you feel yourself getting careless, drive yourself harder and try to do better with each shot, concentrating on hitting the ball in the center of the racket and with more pace.

Usually a player gets sloppy when he is bored with the game because his opponent is not good enough. In that case the answer is to concentrate even more.

What is the best way to handle anger?

There are many reasons for getting angry, but for the most part it is caused by disgust over your errors or brooding over what you consider a bad call. You must realize that anger destroys concentration. If you play angry, you usually end up defeating yourself because instead of thinking about hitting the ball your mind is on the cause of your anger.

I know a great deal about anger because I am an angry player when I am competing. And I am probably one of the few players who was helped by anger because I turned it inward. It helped me concentrate more.

I never allowed my temper to defeat me. I just punished the ball by hitting it even harder, and to do that I had to concentrate even more. Result: I played better because I was trying harder with total concentration.

So, I feel that if you can handle your anger during competition it may indeed help you win. Just turn your anger inward and then let it loose on the ball.

If you get angry during a game it is better not to advertise it. Nothing pleases your opponent more than to see you throw a racket, stamp your feet, or complain about a call. You should try to act unconcerned and force yourself to forget whatever it is that has upset you. You can concentrate on only one thing when you are on the court—defeating your opponent.

How should I handle bad calls?

When you are playing a tournament match you must accept the word of the linesman. There's enough strain on you in competition without your also trying to call shots.

If you are in a game with someone who consistently calls liners out, you can make jokes about it. You can say to him, "Hell, I can't play the ball close to the line against you because you think liners are out" or you can say, "From now on I'm going to hit the ball right straight down the middle so you'll know it's good."

Most people are not cheaters—they are hopers. They hope the ball is out and they get so keyed up during a point that when they see a ball traveling in the air they hope it will land out. When it lands close to the line, they call it out because that's the way they hoped it would be.

If an opponent is consistently giving you bad calls, there's no sense in getting upset about it and letting him get the best of you. It's just not worth it. Go out and find another opponent. Cheaters tend to hang themselves in the end because the word gets out on them and players begin to avoid them.

I always give the benefit of the doubt to my opponents. The thing I really enjoy is the game—getting out on the court and facing the challenge of hitting the ball. Winning has never been all that important to me in practice games, and consequently I have never been under pressure from calls. Having given the benefit of the doubt to my opponents in practice, I could afford to be generous when I got into tournament play because I automatically got a better result from the lines-man.

If there's really any doubt about a point in social tennis, it's my feeling that the point should be replayed.

Why is it that in matches between players of apparently equal ability one of them seems to win more often?

It usually happens because the one who is psychologically convinced he is going to win will wind up winning. He just visualizes himself winning that last point and he enters the match with a positive attitude while his opponent is more doubtful about the outcome and thinks he "may" win.

How can a player maintain a positive attitude if he is losing?

This is where psychology and bluffing play a big part in tennis. You never want to let your opponent know when he has you on the run. You don't throw your racket or start to swear under your breath. If you are getting trimmed you should say to yourself, "This fellow has played the last few games pretty well but he's not that good and I know I'm better than he is." Instead of tightening up and playing more cautiously, lengthen your swing and hit out more. I know a player who starts to whistle or hum when he's under pressure, giving the outward impression at least that he is in control of himself.

What is the best way to handicap the better player?

You can limit him to one serve while the weaker player serves twice. This is good for the stronger player because it forces him to concentrate more and gives the weaker player a slight edge.

Every game can be started at 15-love in favor of the weaker player.

Or, you can have the better player hit to the singles court while the lesser player hits to the doubles court, a system that also makes for better physical competition.

What should be my mental attitude if I am the better player?

Concentrate more. You are still playing against the ball and you still have a target on the other side of the court. Use the occasion to practice and groove your strokes mentally and physically at a slower pace; this will improve your overall game.

If you are in a match you must concentrate even harder to try to win every point.

What is the best way to play against someone who is better?

Relax. Hit out and do the very best you can with every shot. The pressure is on your opponent, who knows he is better, and may therefore get careless. That's why there are frequent upsets in tournament tennis, with a low seed defeating a top seed. The lower-ranked player has nothing to lose so he just hits out, putting pressure on his opponent.

Concentrate on playing every shot as well as possible, although if you're down 40-love there's no point in running yourself ragged.

6.
DURING
AND AFTER
THE GAME

How much water should I drink between games?

Drink as much as you can without getting bloated. I believe in replenishing what the body has used up.

When I play in a hot, dry climate like Las Vegas, I probably sip a pint of water during a set. Most often I just soak a towel in water and then put my face in it to cool off. I also try to breathe a little moisture into my nostrils to lubricate my system.

How often should balls be changed during a match?

A good practice for the average player is to try to play with new balls every two sets.

What do you recommend for a player who has perspired and must sit around waiting to play again?

If you sit around in your wet shirt you will get chills even if it's a nice warm day. And when you go back to play you'll be stiff and tense.

Long ago I developed the habit of carrying an

extra shirt or two in my bag, and I suggest that's what you do if you have to sit out a few games. Nothing will refresh you more than a clean, dry shirt.

Try it. You'll like it.

Do you suggest a shower immediately after playing?

Indeed I do. A brisk, lukewarm shower will help eliminate colds, sniffles, and, most of all, stiffness. When you come out of the shower stay bundled up warmly until your system begins to adjust to the temperature.

And if there's time, a short nap will do wonders for you. Lie down anyplace you can and let your body benefit and recuperate from the exercise.

Do you have any suggestions for avoiding muscle strains and back problems?

From my experience, a lot of the muscle strains and back problems people complain about are due to activities other than tennis. These problems are aggravated and brought to light during a game because of all the movement and activity.

Very often a person with a physical problem will take up tennis and, trying to favor a tender area, he will create a faulty swing which further strains the tender area and may weaken another part of his body.

If you feel that a strain or physical problem is being caused by tennis, you should ask a pro to watch you play and look for a movement which may be causing your problem. If it persists, however, see your doctor.

What is the cause of tennis elbow?

Tennis elbow is actually an injury to a muscle or tendon and is usually brought on by a faulty stroke. Instead of swinging at the ball and letting the racket head do most of the work, some people try to muscle the ball over the net, sustaining much of the shock of impact in their arm and elbow.

Some of the top players have had tennis elbow at one time or another and it is very painful. I had a tennis elbow myself some years ago after playing in New Zealand on a fast indoor floor, under bad lighting and with a pressureless ball. Instead of getting into position and getting my racket back to generate the pace to drive the ball, I found myself slapping at a lot of returns, partly because I couldn't see the ball clearly and partly because the floor was so fast that the ball was too heavy. As a result, I couldn't develop enough forward motion to go through the ball. It felt like a sledgehammer when it hit my racket and the shock jarred my elbow.

How can tennis elbow be cured?

The best way is to stop playing for however long it takes the pain to go away. Certainly it is wise to see your doctor for his recommendation.

125

Some pros, including Rod Laver, Billie Jean King and me, use heat, because we have to continue playing. I got a heating pad with a thermostat which I turned up to a high position. Then I wrapped it around my arm like a sleeve and plugged it in every time I was sitting still, reading the paper, watching television, eating a meal, or watching other matches. My arm was tender and sore, almost painful, whenever I went out to play, but not as painful as it would have been if I hadn't applied heat.

7.
FOR
PLAYERS
PAST
FORTY

You have probably noticed that I consistently refer to the person on the other side of the net as your opponent, someone who is battling you with all the strength, know-how, and talent he has at his disposal. Once you are in competition you are waged in a small-scale battle, but it's not with an enemy and it's not a matter of life or death. Tennis is a game of points, and win, lose, or draw, your life won't have changed one iota after a match. Your wife and family will still love you and you'll still have your job. There will always be another day for you to win.

Your idols should not be players like Stan Smith, who is in his late twenties, or Rod Laver and Ken Rosewall, who are in their mid-thirties. Admire them, but don't try to emulate them.

The players you want to study are men like Frank Sedgman, Pancho Segura, Bobby Riggs, and Frank Parker, who were champions at the same time that you were at your athletic peak. They still play a superb game of tennis, making up in consistency and accuracy what they have lost over the years in speed of foot and reflexes.

Professional tennis is a young man's game, as are most other competitive sports, including golf.

In the early fifties I could drive a ball 270 yards down the fairway. Today, I have to be satisfied with maybe 230 or 240 yards. But I enjoy golf just as I love tennis, and I love tennis as much today as I did during the twenty years I played competitively.

I believe that tennis is a good healthy way of life, especially for the businessman who is under nervous tension at his job. The pressures of life won't affect you quite as much if you exercise, and even a little exercise is better than none.

As I've said before, I know successful businessmen who say they don't have time to play tennis a couple of times a week, but I also know that every successful man can and does make time for the things he really wants to do. You can play tennis during your lunch hour or you can get up an hour earlier and start your day off with a game, or you can play in the evening under lights and go to bed an hour later and sleep the better for it.

But there are certain concessions that the older player has to make if he wants to enjoy and benefit from his tennis games.

DRESS WARMLY BEFORE AND AFTER GAMES. I remember when I was a youngster, my mom used to yell at me to put on a sweater and I'd shout back, "Oh, Mom, I don't need it." Then I'd run out of the house all hot and sweaty, but I rarely got a cold and don't recall ever being stiff.

Today when I warm up before a game, I shed the layers of clothing only when I begin to perspire freely. When I'm finished playing, I dress warmly again and take a shower as soon as possible. I don't dare go into an air-conditioned clubhouse in shorts and a shirt just after playing because I know I will probably get stiff or catch cold.

THE KEY TO YOUR GAME SHOULD BE PERCENTAGE PLAY. Percentage play is a basic part of the game strategy of most past champions. As a matter of fact their biggest problems stem from keeping the ball in play too long.

The secret of percentage play is to not try for winners. Just try to keep the ball in play, putting pressure on your opponent to make the winning shots.

Years ago I could virtually turn my back after hitting certain shots because they were almost sure winners. That's not so today, when I don't have the physical strength and stamina to hit winners consistently. Now I sometimes have to make two or three shots to win such points.

USE A LIGHTER RACKET. Chances are your hand and fingers are not strong enough to quickly maneuver the racket you used three years ago, at least for any length of time.

PREPARE EARLIER. Your reflexes slow down a bit each year, so you must give more thought to moving after the ball from the moment you see it in flight. Be ready to stroke it when it reaches you by turning your body and racket sideways and parallel to the flight of the ball.

CONCENTRATE. Leave your worries at the office. When you are on the tennis court, forget everything else.

Your eyesight is probably not as keen as it used to be. You may tend to see the ball a little less clearly, so you must concentrate even harder, focusing on the ball all the while you make contact and being certain to hit it in the center of the racket.

Lean into the ball. Keep in mind, as your racket is ready to swing at the ball, that you lean into the stroke by transferring your weight to your front foot.

Evaluate the worth of every point. If you're down love-40, it's silly to wear yourself out on that point when you will probably lose the game anyway. It is wiser to use the next point to try to tire your opponent out. Hit drop shots, lobs, and angle shots. You will probably lose the game, but you may win the match because you took a breather and decided to run him a bit. You'll never see a smart older player burn himself out trying to get an impossible shot, even if it is almost within reach, because he knows that if he overextends himself he will be huffing and puffing during the next few points, possibly the next few games.

Don't let anybody rush you. Develop an even tempo of movement, somewhere between running and slow motion. Do everything at the pace you can handle best. If your opponent is impatient, let him get uptight, but never fall into the trap of doing things at his tempo.

Never run to the point of exhaustion. If you do you're going to be the first one who ends up saying, "Why the hell am I doing this to myself?"

Take breathers when you need them. There are lots of tricks you can use to enable yourself to catch your breath and get back into a game. Tie and untie your shoelaces. Go after the balls a trifle slower. Throw up a few lobs. Train your dog to walk slowly across the court at certain moments.

I know a man in Beverly Hills who deliberately drops his racket as a signal for his wife to call

him to the telephone. He gets a breather and upsets his opponent. I don't approve of the tactic but
I appreciate the reason for it.

When changing courts during a match, you are
entitled to sit down for a few moments. Take advantage of every rest period even though your
opponent may rush to the other side. Chances are
he's rushing because he's winning. Maybe you can
engage him in conversation and get him to sit
down with you.

RELAX BETWEEN POINTS. Tighten up and go for
the shot during the point, but stay relaxed at all
other times. That is the secret of lasting power.

DEVELOP YOUR STRONG SHOTS EVEN MORE. As
we've said earlier, it's important for every player
to work on his strength, but it's even more important for the older player. You should have one or
two shots that you can always depend on. If they're
consistently good, your opponent will generally try
to avoid placing the ball in a position for you to
make the shot, thereby putting additional pressure
on him.

HAVE A RELIABLE SECOND SERVE. A cardinal rule
of tennis is to never double fault. You are giving
the point away instead of making your opponent
work for it.

USE MORE DECEPTION ON YOUR SHOTS. Lean forward into the ball so it looks as though you are
going down the line. Then, about the time you
sense your opponent is balanced that way, hit the
ball cross-court. When you're at net, fake to one
direction or another. Try to trick your opponent into
hitting where he thinks you were (and still are).

WORK AT STAYING PHYSICALLY FIT. You must

work twice as hard to stay physically fit at forty as you did at twenty, when fitness seemed to come naturally.

Most men can be much more fit than they believe possible, but they must work at it. I think the greatest inspiration for a man of any age is to watch some of the senior events taking place around the country. He will see men his own age and older competing and in fantastic condition. Any man who is past forty, however, should have frequent physical checkups and coordinate any strenuous physical training program with his doctor.

8.
SURFACES

Most indoor surfaces tend to have good color so the ball stands out clearly. Balls tend to bounce lower on wood than on concrete so the game is usually a trifle slower, giving the defensive player a better chance to run the ball down.

If you play indoors in a tent during the winter you should realize that the ball travels slower and drops earlier because the air is a trifle heavier. You therefore will probably have to make some adjustment. Hit a little higher to get depth and a little harder to get pace.

In an extremely large indoor facility such as Madison Square Garden, the air is thinner and the ball will travel as it normally does outdoors. In the Garden, for example, I estimate that the ball traveling from one end of the court to the other will fly about 2 or 3 feet farther than in the average indoor arena.

Most indoor facilities have good lighting, which may make playing inside very much like playing in the sun. If you are serving or watching an overhead, don't look directly into the light; either look past it or position yourself so that you don't have to look into it.

Outdoors

Concrete courts allow for a full test of the player's ability. The bounce of the ball is uniform on any given shot and a hard serve will scoot. A fast concrete court favors the player who wants to get to the net quickly and likes to run for the liners. Slower courts tend to favor the baseline player.

Concrete is a little hard on the legs, however, so players must learn to use their knees more to cushion the shock as they start, stop, and run.

Clay and composition courts are basically the same. Composition courts favor the defensive player because the footing is so bad that a player may have to slide 2 or 3 feet on the surface to get into position to hit the ball. If your opponent gets to the net and you can get him out of position, he usually doesn't have time to scramble for the next shot.

Because of the difficult footing, most players on composition courts tend to play from the baseline and rush the net when they are certain of making a put-away shot.

Vary your game to the conditions. Shorten your strokes on a fast court and play more steadily on a slow court.

As a professional I find that games on clay courts tend to be boring. The surface slows the tempo down and the player with the most patience and endurance is likely to be the winner. It will take more effort on your part and 25 percent additional concentration to play well on clay, which is a favored surface in Europe because it dries so quickly after rain.

I recall when I was national champion and went east for the first time to defend my title. My home court then was cement, and you got satisfaction when you hit a ball and the pace of the game was fast. But in the East, the game was played on clay and my service was not really as effective. During one match I lost the first set 6-2 because I blasted every ball that was hit to me. But the ball kept coming back until I made an error. My opponent was letting me beat myself.

During the second set I started to analyze my opponent's game. I soon realized that he was fast enough to return most shots, but that he hit the ball with very little pace while I was overhitting his nothing balls. On the plus side, I was more physically fit than he was, which meant that the longer we played, the better would be my chance of winning.

So I slowed down my shots and quickened my body movement and began to run him by hitting short angle shots. I tried to play more within myself and concentrate on getting each shot over the net. In time I started to wear him down and, eventually, I won the match.

Grass is a beautiful surface for local club games, especially during the months of June and July when there is not much likelihood of rain. Grass is soft and easy on the legs, like playing on a plush pile carpet or golf green.

On most shots the ball tends to float into position, which favors the defensive player, but a really hard-hit ball will stay low and scoot, making it hard to hit a ground stroke. So the offensive player has an occasional advantage if he plays aggressively, which is the only way to play anyhow.

If the grass is green and fresh, the ball will pick up grass stain and get progressively heavier and more difficult to see in flight. After four or five games under such conditions, the player must hit the ball harder and heavier to get the desired effect.

I am not fond of grass for professional tournaments because the ball often bounces erratically, and I believe the only test of skill is when the ball bounces true consistently. During or after a light rain, grass can be treacherously slippery. There is an additional problem for the local club: grass is very expensive to keep up.